RESOLVING GERRYMANDERING

A Manageable Standard

ROBERT SCHAFER

AMERICAN**BAR**ASSOCIATION
Judicial Division

Cover design by Amanda Fry/ABA Design

Printed in the United States of America.

25 24 23 22 21   5 4 3 2 1

Library of Congress Cataloging-in-Publication Data

Names: Schafer, Robert, author.
Title: Resolving gerrymandering / Robert Schafer.
Description: Chicago, Illinois : American Bar Association, [2021] |
    Includes bibliographical references and index. | Summary: "This book
    proposes a manageable standard for resolving gerrymandering without the
    entanglements of justiciability and political questions. The standard
    focuses on the mechanism by which gerrymandering operates, not on the
    outcome. The precedent for this focus is the solution to disparate
    population counts in the one-person, one-vote cases. This focus is
    necessary because any remedy needs to work with other unconstitutional
    inequities (such as income based gerrymandering) as well as ones based
    on partisanship"—Provided by publisher.
Identifiers: LCCN 2021036141 (print) | LCCN 2021036142 (ebook) |
    ISBN 9781639050345 (hardcover) | ISBN 9781639050352 (ebook)
Subjects: LCSH: Apportionment (Election law)—United States. |
    Gerrymandering—United States.
Classification: LCC KF4905 .S33 2021 (print) | LCC KF4905 (ebook) |
    DDC 342.73/053—dc23
LC record available at https://lccn.loc.gov/2021036141
LC ebook record available at https://lccn.loc.gov/2021036142

Discounts are available for books ordered in bulk. Special consideration is given to state bars, CLE programs, and other bar-related organizations. Inquire at Book Publishing, ABA Publishing, American Bar Association, 321 N. Clark Street, Chicago, Illinois 60654-7598.

www.shopABA.org

To the memory of the love of my life, Penelope H. Schafer,
my wife, my partner, and my best friend for fifty years.
1944–2020

Contents

Acknowledgments

Thanks to Keith Roberts for reading a draft of the manuscript, providing encouragement, and shepherding me through the application process at the Judicial Council. I am grateful to Elissa Rabellino for editorial assistance and clarifying comments. Thanks to an anonymous reviewer who raised a number of interesting questions and offered valuable suggestions. Thanks to Karl Schafer for insightful comments on a draft that led to significant improvements. A special thanks to Maura Murnane for her skillful conversion of four colored maps to grayscale images. And last but not least, thanks to Penny Schafer, my life partner, who read several drafts and contributed immensely to an improved outcome, and whose belief in me supported me through her last days with me. Needless to say, responsibility for the result rests with me.

About the Author

Robert Schafer has a BS in physics from Union College, an MS in physics from Yale University, a JD from Harvard Law School, and a PhD in urban planning (with a concentration in economics) from Harvard University. He was an associate professor of city and regional planning at Harvard University. He was one of the founders of the *Harvard Civil Rights–Civil Liberties Law Review* in 1966 and served as its editor in chief in 1967–68. He practiced law for more than thirty years. He is the author of *Inequality: Piketty's Capital in a Nutshell* and *The Suburbanization of Multifamily Housing*, coauthor of an early quantitative analysis of racial and gender discrimination in mortgage lending, *Discrimination in Mortgage Lending*; and coauthor of *Housing America's Elderly*. He is a coeditor of *Housing Urban America*.

Introduction

Gerrymandering is the drawing of political district boundaries for one political faction's benefit. The Supreme Court has considered the constitutionality of gerrymandering on several occasions, culminating with *Rucho v. Common Cause* in 2019. While admitting that it violates the Constitution, the Supreme Court has swung from finding gerrymandering claims to be justiciable (resolvable in a court) to concluding that they are not justiciable because they lack "judicially discoverable and manageable standards for resolving" them, alternatively described as a "political question" (*Baker v. Carr*). *Political question* is a doctrine that holds that certain types of cases should not be settled by the courts. Such cases are often described as nonjusticiable—that is, not resolvable in a court. State courts, however, have addressed gerrymandering claims and adopted remedies to resolve them.

Although usually focused on partisanship, gerrymandering can also be based on income, occupation, age, race, ethnicity, or other characteristics. The analysis presented here is equally applicable to each of these forms of gerrymandering. Since the Supreme Court has developed an approach to racial gerrymandering and the prevalence of partisan gerrymandering, recommendations of this analysis have their practical relevance largely in the area of partisan gerrymandering.

This book proposes a manageable standard for resolving gerrymandering without the entanglements of justiciability and political questions. The standard focuses on the mechanism by which gerrymandering operates, not on the outcome. The precedent for this focus is the solution to disparate population counts in the one-person, one-vote cases. This focus is necessary because any remedy needs to work with other unconstitutional inequities (such as income-based gerrymandering), as well as ones based on partisanship.

Although Congress, at one point, resolved both the one-person, one-vote disparity and gerrymandering, the resolution lay dormant and unenforced, and eventually it disappeared from the statute books. The chief barrier to resolution in court has been the Supreme Court's claim that gerrymandering lacks "judicially discoverable and manageable standards," rendering the issue a "political question" that the judiciary should not try to resolve. What refutes this position is the fact that in cases that challenged population disparities, implementation of the one-person, one-vote standard proved easy despite predictions to the contrary. The same would happen in gerrymandering cases under the suggested approach.

A manageable standard for resolving gerrymandering cases would identify a zone of acceptable districting plans. Modern computer techniques can simulate at least 500 alternative districting plans that satisfy traditional districting criteria: population equality, contiguity, compactness, minimization of census voting district splits, minimization of municipal splits, and compliance with court orders under the Voting Rights Act.

Note: Citations and footnotes are omitted from all quotations in the text.

1

Congressional Districts

Congressional districts are the basis for electing persons to the US House of Representatives. Article I, Section 2, of the US Constitution requires members of the House to be "chosen every second year by the people of the several states" and that the electors in each state shall have the qualifications required for voting for members of the most numerous branch of the state legislature. That section also provides that representatives "shall be apportioned among the several states which may be included in this union, according to their respective numbers, which shall be determined by adding to the whole number of free persons, including those bound to service for a term of years, and excluding Indians not taxed, three fifths of all other Persons. The actual Enumeration shall be made . . . within every subsequent term of ten years, in such manner as they shall by law direct." With the adoption of the Thirteenth Amendment to the Constitution in 1865, slavery and involuntary servitude ("except as a punishment for a crime") were eliminated. And in 1868, Section 2 of the Fourteenth Amendment to the Constitution revised the apportionment sentence to read as follows: "Representatives shall be apportioned among the several states according to their respective numbers, counting the whole number of persons in each state, excluding Indians not taxed."

Section 4 of Article I, sometimes called the Elections Clause, sets forth the procedures for electing representatives and senators. It states: "The times, places and manner of holding elections for Senators and Representatives, shall be prescribed in each state by the legislature thereof; but Congress may at any time by law make or alter such regulations, except as to the places of choosing Senators."

Representatives have not always been elected from congressional districts as they are today. For example, the House of Representatives elected in 1802 was apportioned among sixteen states, with six of them electing their members in statewide at-large elections, eight electing members from nonoverlapping, geographically defined districts, and two having only one representative to elect (see Appendix A). In 1842, Congress required that congressional districts be one-member districts "composed of contiguous territory, and containing as nearly as practicable an equal number of inhabitants," which continued in place until the Apportionment Act of 1929. The requirement of single-member congressional districts was reinstated in 1967 (2 U.S.C. § 2c).

The Apportionment Act of 1911 required that representatives "be elected by districts composed of a contiguous and compact territory, and containing as nearly as practical an equal number of inhabitants." This statutory provision became the centerpiece of a challenge to the apportionment of Mississippi's seven congressional districts in the 1930s. In 1932, Mississippi created congressional districts that had populations ranging from 184,000 to 414,000 when the average size based on the 1930 Census was 287,117 (*Broom v. Wood*, the district court opinion). The district court found that "[i]t would be practicable to divide the state into seven districts having compact and contiguous territory with each district having approximately the same number of inhabitants." It ruled in favor of the challenge to the districting plan and enjoined its enforcement. It based its decision on the 1911 apportionment statute. The decision was appealed to the Supreme Court, where it was reversed. What was the reason for the reversal?

The Supreme Court focused on the Apportionment Act of 1911, which by its express terms was limited to representatives that each state was "entitled [to] under this apportionment." The Apportionment Act of 1929, which was the basis of the Mississippi districting, did not contain the 1911 requirement that districts be contiguous, compact, and of equal population. The Court concluded that "the requirements of . . . the Act of 1911 expired by their own limitation. They fell with the apportionment to which they expressly related" (*Wood v. Broom*, 7).

Between 1872 and 1929, congressional districts were required to be composed as nearly as practicable of equal populations, as well as to be

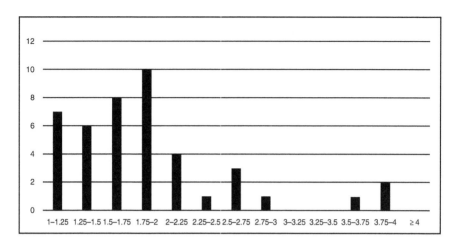

Figure 1 Distribution of the Ratios of Largest to Smallest Congressional Districts, 1928.

Source: Appendix 1 to the Court's opinion in *Colegrove v. Green,* 328 U.S. 529 (1946).

composed of contiguous territory and, after 1901, compact. But according to a report by the Congressional Research Service, "these standards were never enforced if the states failed to meet them" (Crocker, 4). This can be seen clearly from the population disparities between the largest- and smallest-populated districts in each state for 1928, just prior to the adoption of the Apportionment Act of 1929. The distribution of the ratios of the largest- to the smallest-populated congressional districts is summarized in Figure 1. If the requirement of equal populations as nearly as practicable were complied with, all the ratios for the forty-three states with more than one congressional district would be clustered near the value of 1.0. But only seven were close, being less than 1.25. Twelve had populations in the most-populated congressional district that were more than two times as large as the smallest-populated congressional district in the state.

2

Political Question

The Supreme Court avoided addressing population disparities across congressional districts and across state legislative districts in the same state for many years by characterizing them as political questions; more recently, it refused to address gerrymandering on the same ground. *Political question* is a doctrine that holds that certain types of cases should not be settled by the courts. Such cases are often described as nonjusticiable—that is, not resolvable in a court. While the political question doctrine and the justiciability doctrine are referred to in these terms, it was difficult to discern a consistent rule or set of rules that spelled out anything resembling a doctrine prior to *Baker v. Carr*, decided in 1962. Some understanding of this subject is critical background to the development of districting decisions in the United States. It has been and is often asserted as a reason for the courts to avoid entering into cases and controversies surrounding legislative districting.

The history of the political question doctrine can be divided into three distinct periods of time. The first runs from *Marbury v. Madison* in 1803 to *Pacific States Telephone & Telegraph Co. v. Oregon* in 1912, and may be called the "traditional doctrine." The second period extends from 1912 until *Baker v. Carr* in 1962, a period that is characterized more by confusion than by clarity. The third period starts with *Baker v. Carr* and extends to the present (see Grove).

Under the traditional doctrine, political questions were factual determinations by other branches of the government that the courts did not question in deciding cases. The courts enforced the factual determinations of these political branches. Two things stand out during this period. The deference on political questions did not extend to constitutional claims (apart from dicta in one case, namely *Luther v. Borden*)—that is, the courts were not bound by the determinations of political branches on constitutional issues. And factual determinations on political questions were not a basis for not proceeding with the case or controversy to a decision on the merits—that is, not grounds for dismissal.

Some examples may help. In one case, the recovery of insurance proceeds depended on what government controlled the Falkland Islands (*Williams v. Suffolk Ins. Co.*). The executive branch of the United States had made a determination of what government exercised control over the Falkland Islands. The Supreme Court regarded this as a factual determination by another branch of government that it had to treat as a fact in resolving the dispute between a ship owner and its insurance carrier, whether the executive branch was right or wrong. This fact materially affected the outcome of the dispute. In another case, involving a dispute arising out of the Mexican War, a critical issue was whether at the time of a contract Texas was a part of Mexico (*Kennett v. Chambers*). The Supreme Court treated this as a political question that revolved around when the political branches of the United States recognized Texas as independent from Mexico. Although Texas had declared its independence, the United States did not recognize Texas until several months after the contract in question. As a result, the contract was illegal. Another example is whether a group of Native Americans constituted a "tribe" (*United States v. Holliday*).

The next period starts with the Supreme Court's decision in the *Pacific States* case. During this period, the Supreme Court continued to apply the traditional doctrine but also ventured afield. In 1912, the Supreme Court confronted a claim under the Guarantee Clause. This clause provides that the "United States shall guarantee to every state in this union a republican form of government" (Article IV, section 4). In *Pacific States*, the Oregon voters had adopted a tax on corporations by popular initiative. A business objecting to this law claimed that it violated the Guarantee Clause because it was not adopted by the legislature, the representatives of the people, and hence was inconsistent with a republican form of government. Instead of following prior practice in this area, the Supreme Court held that the enforcement of the Guarantee

Clause was "exclusively committed" to Congress "because of its political character." And the Supreme Court dismissed the businessman's constitutional claim "for want of jurisdiction" (*Pacific States*, 137, 151). The Supreme Court continued to treat claims under the Guarantee Clause as nonjusticiable political questions for the next thirty-five years without finding other constitutional claims to be nonjusticiable as political questions.

Then, two divided decisions created confusion. In the 1939 case of *Coleman v. Miller*, three justices based their votes to dismiss the claim on the ground that the validity of an approval by a state of a proposed amendment to the US Constitution was a political question for Congress to decide. Four other justices based their decision to dismiss the claim on a lack of standing by the plaintiffs. And two dissenting justices would have applied the traditional doctrine.

In 1946, the Supreme Court reviewed a challenge to congressional voting districts in the state of Illinois in *Colegrove v. Green*. Again, only three justices based their votes on a position that the plaintiffs' claim was a nonjusticiable political question that the Constitution conferred on Congress. Three justices dissented, stating that the claim did not present a nonjusticiable political question. The case was decided by seven justices as a result of a vacancy by the death of Chief Justice Stone and the absence of Justice Jackson, who was in Europe as chief prosecutor in the Nuremberg trials. The seventh justice voted to dismiss the complaint for want of equity and in doing so expressed agreement with the dissenters on the issue of justiciability.

It is worthwhile to lay out the facts in *Colegrove v. Green* for later comparison with the post–*Baker v. Carr* cases. Illinois established the boundaries of its congressional districts in 1901 on the basis of the 1900 Census. Illinois did not reapportion its congressional districts to reflect changes in its population and the distribution of its population across the state based on any of the 1910, 1920, 1930, and 1940 Censuses. (Apparently, it did manage to adjust the total number of representatives it was entitled to.) As a result, by the time of this case, congressional districts in Illinois varied in population from 112,116 to 914,000. To be clear, the Supreme Court was aware of all the discrepancies in population between congressional districts in every state, as it attached an appendix to the Court's opinion setting forth the largest- and smallest-populated congressional districts in each state for 1897, 1928, and 1946.

The population figures from the Supreme Court's appendix are presented in Appendix C. The Supreme Court also attached an appendix setting forth maps of the boundaries of congressional districts in four states as examples of prevailing gerrymanders.

Neither *Coleman* nor *Colegrove* stands for a political question doctrine extending beyond the Guarantee Clause. How did it come about that by the middle of the twentieth century, there was widespread espousal of a political question doctrine that described constitutional issues that were outside the Court's jurisdiction? At least one commentator attributes the evolution of this doctrine to legal scholarship, especially the legal process theorists (Grove, 1947–59). Legal process theorists believed that judicial discretion could be limited through procedure; reasoned decision-making combined with procedural doctrines like standing, ripeness, and mootness would define the area of judicial authority, and within that area constitutional decisions were proper. The political question doctrine fit nicely into this framework as a procedural limit on the jurisdiction of the judiciary, even though the case law did not support it. Over time, the legal process view of the political question doctrine was adopted by jurists and found its way into judicial decisions.

By 1962, much of the legal world operated on the assumption that there was a political question doctrine that acted as a significant limitation on the power of the courts to make decisions on the merits in cases raising constitutional issues. Yet, the concept of the judiciary as the final arbiter of constitutional issues was well established in the decisions of the Supreme Court. This conflict between a school of thought and the Court's decisions came to a head in *Baker v. Carr*.

Baker v. Carr involved the apportionment of the Tennessee legislature. The last time Tennessee had reapportioned the two houses of its legislature was in 1901 on the basis of the US Census of 1900. By 1961, the population of Tennessee had grown and was distributed across the Tennessee geography quite differently than it had been in 1901. The population of the state grew from 2,020,616 to 3,587,089, and the number of registered voters rose from 487,380 to 2,092,891. The plaintiffs claimed that the failure of Tennessee to reapportion its state legislature violated the Equal Protection Clause of the Fourteenth Amendment to the US Constitution. The federal district court dismissed the complaint in apparent reliance on the legal process theory of justiciability. The Supreme Court reversed.

Baker v. Carr is often thought of as the leading case for the one-person, one-vote decisions, but in fact it did not set that standard. *Baker v. Carr* only dealt with procedural issues: jurisdiction, standing, and justiciability. It held by a 6–2 vote that the court had jurisdiction, plaintiffs had standing, and the challenge to apportionment presented no nonjusticiable "political question." The latter is the focus of the following discussion and is the centerpiece of the case.

After a detailed review of the Court's cases addressing the "political question" concept, the Court arrived at a new political question doctrine. Some call this the *modern doctrine*. It is summarized in the following often-quoted paragraph listing six characteristics of prior political action cases:

> It is apparent that several formulations which vary slightly according to the settings in which the questions arise may describe a political question, although each has one or more elements which identify it as essentially a function of the separation of powers. Prominent on the surface of any case held to involve a political question is found a textually demonstrable constitutional commitment of the issue to a coordinate political department; or a lack of judicially discoverable and manageable standards for resolving it; or the impossibility of deciding without an initial policy determination of a kind clearly for nonjudicial discretion; or the impossibility of a court's undertaking independent resolution without expressing lack of the respect due coordinate branches of government; or an unusual need for unquestioning adherence to a political decision already made; or the potentiality of embarrassment from multifarious pronouncements by various departments on one question. (*Baker*, 217)

In leading up to its discussion of prior cases, the Court made its position clear that "it is the relationship between the judiciary and the coordinate branches of the Federal Government, and not the federal judiciary's relationship to the States, which gives rise to the 'political question'" (*Baker*, 210). The Court dealt with *Colegrove v. Green* by noting that four of the seven voting justices had found that the plaintiff's claim was justiciable and not a political question.

The Court then held that none of these characteristics was present in the claim that Tennessee's apportionment was in violation of the

Equal Protection Clause of the Fourteenth Amendment. A key element was that the case did not even involve a coordinate department of the federal government. The following is the Court's assessment of its six characteristics in *Baker v. Carr*:

> A natural beginning is to note whether any of the common characteristics which we have been able to identify and label descriptively are present. We find none: The question here is the consistency of state action with the Federal Constitution. We have no question decided, or to be decided, by a political branch of government coequal with this Court. Nor do we risk embarrassment of our government abroad, or grave disturbance at home if we take issue with Tennessee as to the constitutionality of her action here challenged. Nor need the appellants, in order to succeed in this action, ask the Court to enter upon policy determinations for which judicially manageable standards are lacking. Judicial standards under the Equal Protection Clause are well developed and familiar, and it has been open to courts since the enactment of the Fourteenth Amendment to determine, if on the particular facts they must, that a discrimination reflects *no* policy, but simply arbitrary and capricious action. (*Baker*, 226)

It appears appropriate to refer to this exposition of the political question as a new doctrine and not merely a description of an existing doctrine. To start with, the opinion of the Court asserts that the courts "will not stand impotent before an obvious instance of a manifestly unauthorized exercise of power" (*Baker*, 217). In addition, the Court's opinion treated the presence of a political question as grounds for dismissal. These gut the heart of the traditional doctrines where the courts followed the political determinations as factual matters and proceeded to decide the cases on their merits, taking those determinations as facts. Moreover, the Court took control of the constitutional issues because the Court would decide whether the six characteristics were or were not present in any case. As a result, the Court would decide which institution would decide a constitutional question. It was the ultimate arbiter of the Constitution. In this light, *Baker v. Carr* can be viewed as a case that enhances judicial power, not one that imposes limits on it.

The meaning of *Baker v. Carr* for voting rights is that it removed the obstacle of the nonjusticiability of a political question from blocking the consideration of constitutional issues in legislative districting cases. As a result, the Court proceeded to develop and implement the requirement that legislative districts within a state have equal populations, the now-familiar requirement of one-person, one-vote.

3

One Person, One Vote

What were the population disparities across congressional districts at the time that *Baker v. Carr* was being decided? Figure 2 shows the distribution of the ratios of the largest-populated congressional district to the smallest-populated congressional district within each of the forty-two states with two or more congressional districts for the Eighty-Eighth Congress. (The other states either had only one representative or utilized at-large elections, which were permitted at the time.) The Eighty-Eighth Congress served from January 3, 1963, to January 3, 1965. These population numbers come from the 1960 Census, and at least twenty of the states had been redistricted. The distribution of these ratios did not appreciably change between 1928 and 1962. (In 1928, there were forty-three states with at least two congressional districts.) While seven states in 1928 had ratios below 1.25, only four did so in 1962. In addition, twelve states had ratios of 2 or more in 1928 and thirteen had such ratios in 1962. If a state had created congressional districts with equal populations within that state, the ratio for that state would be 1.0.

In 1964, after *Baker v. Carr*, the Supreme Court confronted a pattern of Georgia's congressional districts not unlike the ones presented in *Colegrove v. Green* and *Wood v. Broom*. In the Georgia case (*Wesberry v. Sanders*), the population of the state divided by its ten congressional districts was 394,312 according to the 1960 Census, and the population of congressional districts ranged from 272,154 to 823,680. These districts were created in 1931. Based on the 1960 Census, the difference between the largest- and the smallest-populated congressional districts as a percentage of the mathematical ideal (state population divided by

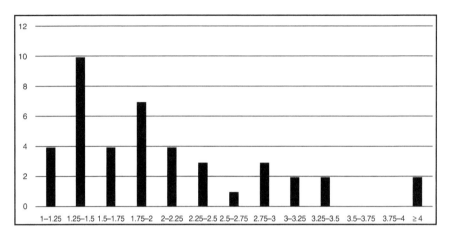

Figure 2   Distribution of the Ratios of Largest- to Smallest-Populated Congressional Districts, Eighty-Eighth Congress (1963–1964)

Source: US Bureau of the Census, Population of Congressional Districts for 88th Congress, April 1, 1960, 1960 Census of Population: Suppl. Rep. No. PC(S1)-26 (August 6, 1962).

the number of congressional districts) was 140 percent, and the ratio of the largest- to the smallest-populated congressional district was 3.03 (*Wesberry v. Sanders*, 2). Despite finding that the populations of Georgia's congressional districts were "grossly out of balance," a majority of the district court dismissed the challenge to this apportionment. In doing so, it based its decision on what the *Wesberry v. Sanders* Supreme Court decision referred to as "Mr. Justice Frankfurter's minority opinion in *Colegrove v. Green*, an opinion stating that challenges to apportionment of congressional districts raised only 'political' questions, which were not justiciable" (*Wesberry*, 3–4). As was discussed above, a majority of the justices voting in *Colegrove v. Green* found that the case was justiciable and rejected Justice Frankfurter's opinion of nonjusticiability due to its being a "political question." The Supreme Court dealt swiftly with the "political question" argument by reviewing *Baker v. Carr* and finding that the reasons leading to the conclusions in *Baker v. Carr* were "equally persuasive" in *Wesberry v. Sanders* (*Wesberry*, 6). The following is what the Court had to say about Justice Frankfurter's argument:

> Mr. Justice Frankfurter's *Colegrove* opinion contended that Art. I, § 4, of the Constitution had given Congress "exclusive authority" to protect the right of citizens to vote for Congressmen, but we made

it clear in *Baker* that nothing in the language of that article gives support to a construction that would immunize state congressional apportionment laws which debase a citizen's right to vote from the power of courts to protect the constitutional rights of individuals from legislative destruction. . . . The right to vote is too important in our free society to be stripped of judicial protection by such an interpretation of Article I. This dismissal can no more be justified on the ground of "want of equity" than on the ground of "non-justiciability." We therefore hold that the District Court erred in dismissing the complaint. (*Wesberry*, 6–7)

Moving on to the merits, the Court in *Wesberry v. Sanders* applied its famous one-person, one-vote rule to apportionment of congressional districts. Here is the Court's reasoning:

We hold that, construed in its historical context, the command of Art. I, § 2, that Representatives be chosen "by the People of the several States" means that as nearly as is practicable one man's vote in a congressional election is to be worth as much as another's. This rule is followed automatically, of course, when Representatives are chosen as a group on a statewide basis, as was a widespread practice in the first 50 years of our Nation's history. It would be extraordinary to suggest that in such statewide elections the votes of inhabitants of some parts of a State, for example, Georgia's thinly populated Ninth District, could be weighted at two or three times the value of the votes of people living in more populous parts of the State, for example, the Fifth District around Atlanta. We do not believe that the Framers of the Constitution intended to permit the same vote-diluting discrimination to be accomplished through the device of districts containing widely varied numbers of inhabitants. (*Wesberry*, 7–8)

The *Wesberry v. Sanders* opinion rests on the interpretation of the Elections Clause in Article I, Section 4, of the Constitution. Although the complaint in this case raised other bases for objecting to the redistricting plan (the Due Process, Equal Protection, and Privileges and Immunities clauses of the Fourteenth Amendment), the Court stated in a footnote that it did not reach those claims (*Wesberry v. Sanders*, 8, footnote 10). By the terms of the Fourteenth Amendment, these clauses protect against state action. Since the states are the ones implementing the procedure for electing representatives, these clauses are applicable. In addition, the Supreme Court held in 1954 that the Due Process Clause of the Fifth Amendment includes the concept of equal protection contained in the Fourteenth Amendment and, as such, applies to the federal government as well as the states (see *Bolling v. Sharpe*). Therefore, the equal protection of the law applies to acts of Congress under Article I regulating the electoral process.

It is noteworthy that the one-person, one-vote rule in case law did not arise out of a state legislative or congressional districting decision. Rather, it came about in a 1963 case examining the system of selecting primary candidates for statewide office in Georgia (*Gray v. Sanders*). Georgia had a system for selecting primary candidates based on the outcomes of the vote on a county-by-county basis. Counties were assigned one or more units, and the candidate who won the popular vote in a county won the units allocated to that county. The candidate who won the most units became the nominee. The problem arose because the allocation of units to counties bore no sensible relationship to the populations of the counties. In fact, the allocation was such that rural counties with very few people could determine the outcome. For example, Fulton County had 14.11 percent of Georgia's 1960 population and only 1.46 percent of the unit votes. On the other hand, Echols County had 0.05 percent of the state's 1960 population and 0.48 percent of the unit votes. One vote of an Echols County voter was equal to the votes of 99 Fulton County voters. The Supreme Court in an 8–1 decision stated that the "concept of 'we the people' visualizes no preferred class of voters" (*Gray v. Sanders*, 379–80). The Court held that "[t]he conception of political equality from the Declaration of Independence, to Lincoln's Gettysburg Address, to the Fifteenth, Seventeenth, and Nineteenth Amendments can mean only one thing—one person, one vote" (*Gray*, 381).

Even more interesting is the fact that the one-person, one-vote standard is the same requirement that the Apportionment Act of 1911 imposed on congressional districts. It appears that the guidance to this standard came from congressional legislation. And perhaps it should do so once again in the gerrymandering cases to be discussed below.

Returning to the congressional districting issue, the remaining question is, how precise does the equality of population across congressional districts in a state have to be to satisfy the ruling in *Wesberry v. Sanders?* What does "as nearly as practicable" mean? This inquiry was definitively answered in *Kirkpatrick v. Preisler,* a 1969 decision involving congressional districting in Missouri. The case reviews Missouri's second attempt to comply with *Wesberry v. Sanders.* Absolute equality of population among its ten congressional districts would require each district to have 431,981 persons, according to the 1960 Census. Under the redistricting plan being reviewed by the Supreme Court, the least-populous congressional district would have a population 12,260 persons below this standard of equality, and the most-populous congressional district would have a population 13,542 persons above this standard of equality. The range of divergence from equality went from 2.84 percent below to 3.13 percent above the "mathematical ideal" (*Kirkpatrick v. Preisler,* 528–29). In percentage terms, the difference between the largest- and the smallest-populated proposed congressional districts was 5.97 percent of the mathematical average, and the ratio of the largest-populated to the smallest-populated proposed congressional district was 1.061 percent.

The Supreme Court noted three findings made by the district court: the Missouri General Assembly had not relied on the 1960 Census; the General Assembly had rejected a plan that provided smaller population variances; and by switching some counties, it would have been easy to reduce the population variance. The district court threw out the Missouri plan. On appeal, Missouri's primary argument was that the variations from the mathematical ideal should be considered de minimis and therefore acceptable. The Supreme Court rejected this argument, holding that the "as nearly as practicable" standard "requires that the State make a good-faith effort to achieve precise mathematical equality. Unless population variances among congressional districts are shown to have resulted despite such effort, the State must justify each variance, no matter how small" (*Kirkpatrick,* 530–31).

What did Missouri offer as justifications for the variances in its plan, and what did the Supreme Court conclude about them? Missouri offered six justifications; the Supreme Court found them all lacking. Three of its offered justifications were rejected as inconsistent with the concept of equal representation for equal numbers of persons. These were that the variances were necessary to avoid fragmenting distinct economic or social areas, they arose out of legislative interplay in legislative compromise, and they were necessary to avoid fragmenting local political jurisdictions. Missouri also offered as a justification that it was adjusting the districts to reflect variances in the number of eligible voters, but the Court found its attempt unacceptable, as the state had made no effort to determine the number of eligible voters in each district. (The Court explicitly stated that it was not deciding that apportionment could be based on something other than total population, such as eligible voters.) Missouri also claimed that the variances were due to an effort to project population shifts. According to the Court, any effort along these lines would require predictions "with a high degree of accuracy," and it found that Missouri's effort fell short of this test (*Kirkpatrick*, 535). Missouri's last justification was that the variances resulted from its efforts to achieve geographical compactness, which was rejected as being unnecessary in light of modern methods of transportation and communication.

The meaning of "as nearly as practicable" in congressional districting was again before the Supreme Court in *Karcher v. Daggett*, involving the drawing of the New Jersey congressional district boundaries after the 1980 Census. The proposed congressional districts varied in population size from 523,798 to 527,472, with a mathematical average of 526,059. The difference between the smallest- and the largest-populated districts was 0.6984 percent of the average. The ratio of the largest- to the smallest-populated district was 1.01. The state legislature had before it other plans with less population variance from the average. The district court held that the population variances were not "unavoidable despite a good-faith effort to achieve absolute equality" and that the population variances had not been shown to be justifiable (*Karcher v. Daggett*, 729). The Supreme Court in a 5–4 decision affirmed a three-judge district court panel's decision declaring the New Jersey redistricting plan unconstitutional. The only issue in the case was an argument by the proponents of the plan that if the plan was within the statistical imprecision of the census (e.g., predictable undercount), the plan was in effect the equivalent of mathematical equality. The Supreme Court rejected this argument, finding that it was no more than a dressed-up

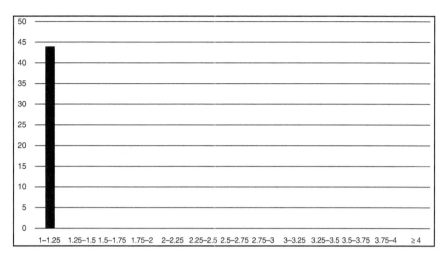

Figure 3   Distribution of the Ratios of Largest- to Smallest-Populated Congressional Districts, Ninety-Third Congress (1973–1974).

Source: US Bureau of the Census, 1970 Population of Congressional Districts for the 93rd Congress, Suppl. Rep. No. PC(S1)-28 (October 1972).

de minimis proposal wrapped up in an "illusion of rationality and predictability" (*Karcher*, 735).

What was the effect of *Wesberry v. Sanders* on the population of congressional districts, and how long did it take to conform congressional districts to its standard? It is worth noting that the two dissents in *Baker v. Carr* expressed concerns over how to formulate a remedy for implementing the decision. Some might say they ranted and raved about the difficulty of doing so. Yet the standard that evolved seems very easy to apply and quite straightforward. The first census after the one-person, one-vote cases was in 1970, and the first Congress to be affected by them was the Ninety-Third Congress, serving from January 3, 1973, to January 3, 1975. The implementation was swift. Figure 3 shows the distribution of the ratios of the largest-populated to the smallest-populated congressional districts in each of the forty-four states with two or more congressional districts. The categories are the same as those in Figures 1 and 2. The comparison of the Ninety-Third Congress to these earlier ones is striking. By the Ninety-Third Congress, all states had ratios below 1.25. In fact, the result was even better than that, with no ratio over 1.126. Twenty-seven states had ratios below 1.01, and six more states had ratios between 1.1 and 1.2. And it got even better. By the 115th Congress, serving from January 3, 2017, to January 3, 2019, twenty-two of the forty-three states with at least two congressional districts had either no population differences (only one state) between their largest-populated and smallest-populated congressional districts or a difference of only one person; thirty-eight states had a ratio of their largest-populated to their smallest-populated congressional district below 1.0001. The three states with the highest ratios were Maryland (1.016), Virginia (1.055), and West Virginia (1.007).

4

State Legislative Districts

Baker v. Carr involved the differences in the weight given to voters in state legislative districts; it established that these issues were justiciable but did not address the remedy that would be appropriate. In 1964, the Supreme Court faced this question in the case of *Reynolds v. Sims*. At issue was the apportionment of the two houses of the Alabama State Legislature. The existing apportionment was based on a 1901 plan, which had not been updated. On the basis of the 1960 Census, that plan resulted in 25.1 percent of the state's population electing a majority of the State Senate and 25.7 percent of the state's population electing a majority of the State House. The ratio of the largest Senate district in population to the smallest was 41 to 1, and the ratio of the largest House district in population to the smallest was 16 to 1.

Three days after *Baker v. Carr* was handed down and while the case challenging the Alabama districting was pending, the Alabama State Legislature adopted two alternative redistricting plans: one was a proposed state constitutional amendment and the other was a statutory reapportionment plan (referred to as the Crawford-Webb Act) to take effect if the state constitutional amendment was not adopted by the voters. Under the proposed constitutional amendment, 19.4 percent of the state's population would elect a majority of the State Senate and 43 percent of the state's population would elect a majority of the State House. The ratio of the largest Senate district in population to the smallest would have been 59 to 1, and the ratio of the largest House district in population to the smallest would have been 4.7 to 1. Under the Crawford-Webb Act, 27.6 percent of the state's population would elect a majority of the State Senate, and 37 percent of the state's population would elect a majority of the State House. The ratio of the largest Senate district in population to the smallest would have been 20 to 1, and the ratio of the largest House district in population to the smallest would have been 5 to 1.

The district court rejected all three versions of apportionment of the Alabama State Senate and House. The Supreme Court affirmed in an 8–1 decision. It is important to note that state apportionment cases are different than congressional ones because the congressional ones rely on a provision of the US Constitution that addresses the election of representatives to the US House of Representatives. This Elections Clause is not available in challenges to state apportionment cases, which instead look to the Fourteenth Amendment. The Fourteenth Amendment provides that "[n]o state shall make or enforce any law which shall . . . deny to any person within its jurisdiction the equal protection of the laws." It is interesting to note that in *Karcher v. Daggett*, the New Jersey case requiring mathematical equality, the deciding vote was cast by Justice Stevens, who in a concurring opinion found firmer ground in the Equal Protection Clause than in the Elections Clause (*Karcher v. Daggett*, 744).

Claims of violation of the Equal Protection Clause are evaluated by whether the government's action is rationally related to one or more legitimate governmental interests (the rational relationship test) unless the claim relates to a class that is entitled to heightened scrutiny, which requires the governmental interest to be compelling or important. The Supreme Court has applied what has been referred to as "heightened scrutiny" in equal protection cases formally to race, national origin, alienage, sex (but not sexual orientation), and nonmarital parentage (Yoshino, 756). In the absence of a racial claim, claims that population disparities across legislative districts in a state violate the Equal Protection Clause are evaluated under the rational relationship test.

While pointing out that *Gray v. Sanders* dealt with statewide elections and *Wesberry v. Sanders* involved congressional districts, the Supreme Court stated in *Reynolds v. Sims* that these cases, though not dispositive, "clearly established that the fundamental principle of representative government in this country is one of equal representation for equal numbers of people, without regard to race, sex, economic status, or place of residence within a state" (*Reynolds v. Sims*, 560–61). Then it stated the problem facing it in *Reynolds* as ascertaining "whether there are any constitutionally cognizable principles which would justify departures from the basic standard of equality among voters in the apportionment of seats in state legislatures" (*Reynolds*, 561). The Supreme Court concluded that treating the votes of some voters as having a substantially different weight than others was a violation of the Equal Protection Clause of the Fourteenth Amendment.

The Supreme Court reasoned,

> Any suggested criteria for the differentiation of citizens are insufficient to justify any discrimination, as to the weight of their votes, unless relevant to the permissible purposes of legislative apportionment. Since the achieving of fair and effective representation for all citizens is concededly the basic aim of legislative apportionment, we conclude that the Equal Protection Clause guarantees the opportunity for equal participation by all voters in the election of state legislators. Diluting the weight of votes *because of place of residence* impairs basic constitutional rights under the Fourteenth Amendment just as much as invidious discriminations based upon factors such as race or economic status. (*Reynolds*, 565–66; emphasis added)

This was followed by its holding.

> We hold that, as a basic constitutional standard, the Equal Protection Clause requires that the seats in both houses of a bicameral state legislature must be apportioned on a population basis. Simply stated, an individual's right to vote for state legislators is unconstitutionally impaired when its weight is in a substantial fashion diluted when compared with votes of citizens living in other parts of the State. (*Reynolds*, 568)

In arriving at its holding, the Supreme Court rejected the argument that the analogy to the federal legislature (i.e., the election of United States senators being by state and not by population) justified a similar approach in the states. The difference lay in the thirteen original states being sovereign entities joining together to form a unified government. The sovereign entity reasoning does not apply to the states within that unified government, but only to the national legislative compromise spelled out in the US Constitution.

It is noteworthy, however, that the language of the holding describes a "substantial" dilution of the weight of an individual's vote, which appears less demanding than the standard applicable to congressional apportionment, though the Supreme Court used some of the same language that appears in the congressional districting case. *Wesberry v. Sanders* utilized the phrase "as nearly as is practicable." And this same phrase appears in *Reynolds v. Sims.* The Supreme Court stated that its *Reynolds* holding meant that "the Equal Protection Clause requires that a State make an honest and good faith effort to construct districts, in both houses of its legislature, as nearly of equal population as is practicable" (*Reynolds*, 577). However, the Supreme Court's opinion in *Reynolds* went on to discuss factors that a state may take into account, such as local political boundaries. The Supreme Court then stated that "the overriding objective must be substantial equality of population among the various districts, so that the vote of any citizen is approximately equal in weight to that of any other citizen in the State" (*Reynolds*, 579). In addition, it found that "[s]o long as the divergences from a strict population standard are based on legitimate considerations incident to the effectuation of a rational state policy, some deviations from the equal population principle are constitutionally permissible with respect to the apportionment of seats in either or both of the two houses of a bicameral state legislature" (*Reynolds*, 579).

While the progeny of *Wesberry v. Sanders* in congressional districting cases developed into a requirement of near-mathematical equality of population across a state's congressional districts, the progeny of *Reynolds v. Sims* in state legislative districting cases allow considerable deviation from the mathematical ideal of population equality.

The Supreme Court made this distinction between congressional and state legislative redistricting cases explicit in *Mahan v. Howell,* a 1973 case involving the redistricting of the Virginia House of Delegates and Senate. That decision by a 5–3 vote approved a redistricting plan with a ratio of the largest district in population to the smallest district of 1.18 as constitutionally tolerable upon the justification that the state sought to give representation to local political jurisdictions and had achieved this with only one exception. The population difference between the largest- and smallest-populated districts as a percentage of the mathematical ideal was 16 percent.

Also in 1973, the Supreme Court recognized that "minor deviations from mathematical equality among state legislative districts are insufficient to make out a prima facie case of invidious discrimination under the Fourteenth Amendment so as to require justification by the State" (*Gaffney v. Cummings*, 745). *Gaffney* involved a challenge to legislative redistricting in Connecticut that resulted in a population difference between the largest- and smallest-populated districts as a percentage of the mathematical ideal of equality of 7.83 percent, with a ratio of the largest- to the smallest-populated district equal to 1.08.

In 2016, the Supreme Court reviewed its decision standards in apportionment cases. It was clear that the standards applicable to the apportionment of state legislative districts were not as strict as those applicable to congressional districts. Although the Court's discussion was not essential to the case under review, *Evenwel v. Abbott*, it offers a relatively concise summary of the case law on apportionment. The following is what the opinion stated on apportionment review in an 8–0 decision:

> Over the ensuing decades, the Court has several times elaborated on the scope of the one-person, one-vote rule. States must draw congressional districts with populations as close to perfect equality as possible. But, when drawing state and local legislative districts, jurisdictions are permitted to deviate somewhat from perfect population equality to accommodate traditional districting objectives, among them, preserving the integrity of political subdivisions, maintaining communities of interest, and creating geographic compactness. Where the maximum population deviation between the largest and smallest district is less than 10%, the Court has held, a state or local legislative map presumptively complies with the one-person, one-vote rule. Maximum deviations above 10% are presumptively impermissible. (*Evenwel v. Abbott*, 3–4)

The issue in dispute in *Evenwel v. Abbott* involved the question of the population base that jurisdictions must use in making apportionment decisions for state legislative districts. Plaintiffs in that case claimed that Texas must use the voter-eligible population to make apportionment decisions and not the total population that Texas was using. The Supreme Court held that it is permissible for a state to use total population in making apportionment decisions for state legislative districts. Seemingly arguing against its adopted use of total population, Texas argued that it could have used voter-eligible population. But the Court explicitly stated that "we need not and do not resolve whether, as Texas now argues, states may draw districts to equalize voter eligible populations rather than total population" (*Evenwel*, 19).

5

Gerrymandering

The current challenge to fair and democratic elections lies in the abusive use of gerrymandering to affect the legislative representational outcomes of elections. What is gerrymandering? It is the drawing of the boundaries of political districts so that the resulting district or districts benefit some group or disadvantage some other group. The name is derived from a state senate district created in Massachusetts in 1812 by Governor Elbridge Gerry that some thought looked like a salamander, hence *gerrymander*. Gerrymandering is distinct from the one-person, one-vote requirement where one person's vote is given equal weight to another person's vote. In gerrymandering situations, each person's vote is in compliance with the provisions governing the one-person, one-vote requirement. The districts each have the requisite number of persons in them (virtually identical in the case of congressional districts within a state and nearly identical for state legislative districts within a state). Gerrymandering uses voter characteristics and preferences in combination with geography to tilt election outcomes in a particular direction.

Modern-day gerrymandering focuses on winning districts by as close a reliable margin as possible. One strategy for achieving this is to construct districts that give one group a relatively secure chance of winning them by spreading its support across the maximum number of districts. As a result, the favored group can count on winning the majority of the districts, not by large margins but by comfortable ones. The unfavored group would be able to win only a minority of the districts. This is sometimes referred to as *cracking* or *splitting*. The other approach is to concentrate a group's support in a few districts, which they then win by a large margin, while the other group wins more seats in the remaining districts, a practice sometimes referred to as *packing* or *stacking.* Often these strategies are used in combination. The group benefiting is often a political party, but it need not be. It could just as well be classifications by income, occupation, or a host of other criteria about the residents for which modern-day data gathering and processing operations provide the underlying information.

Gerrymandering has been challenged on the grounds that it violates the US Constitution. Three different theories of constitutional violations have been put forth: (a) the requirement that the people elect their representatives (the Elections Clause in Article I, Section 2), (b) the equal protection of the laws guaranteed by the Fourteenth Amendment, and (c) the First Amendment protection of the right to free speech and assembly. (Brief of Common Cause.) The first theory is limited by its language to election of representatives to the US House of Representatives. The other two are equally applicable to congressional and state legislative elections. Most of the challenges to gerrymandering have been based on the claim that the Equal Protection Clause has been violated.

First Amendment theories have appeared only recently. The First Amendment approach argues that gerrymandering burdens protected speech and assembly activity on the basis of the motivating ideology of the speaker (i.e., characteristics of voters identified with an ideology), regulates protected speech and assembly activity on the basis of the identity of the speaker, and penalizes persons for their association with a party or for their expression of political views.

It comes as no surprise that the first gerrymandering case decided by the Supreme Court, *Gomillion v. Lightfoot,* came in the context of racial discrimination. In 1957, the state of Alabama redefined the boundaries of the city of Tuskegee, altering it from the shape of a square to a twenty-eight-sided figure. The boundaries before and after the alteration are shown in Figure 4.

The effect of this alteration was to remove all but four or five black voters from the city of Tuskegee and no white voters. The plaintiffs alleged that the redrawn boundaries discriminated on the basis of race. The district court dismissed the case on procedural grounds without taking evidence on the merits of the complaint. As a result, the Supreme

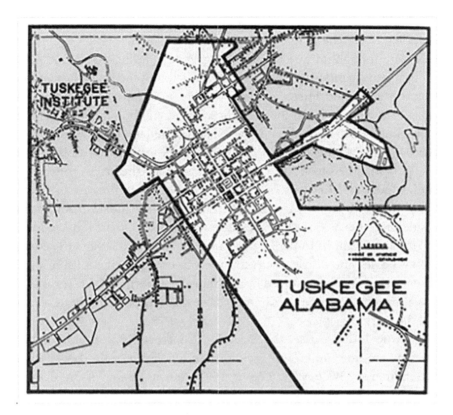

Figure 4 Boundaries of the City of Tuskegee Before and After Redistricting.

Appendix to Opinion of the Court. Chart showing Tuskegee, Alabama, before and after Act 140. The entire area of the square comprised the city prior to Act 140. The irregular, black-bordered figure within the square represents the post-enactment city.

Gomillion v. Lightfoot 363 U.S. 338 (1960).

Court's review is based on the assumption that the allegations could be proven. The Supreme Court stated, "These allegations, if proven, would abundantly establish that Act 140 was not an ordinary geographic redistricting measure even within familiar abuses of gerrymandering" (*Gomillion v. Lightfoot*, 341). And it held by a 9–0 vote that "[w]hen a legislature thus singles out a readily isolated segment of a racial minority for special discriminatory treatment, it violates the Fifteenth Amendment" (*Gomillion*, 346). The Fifteenth Amendment protects the citizens' right to vote against denial or abridgement "on account of race, color, or previous condition of servitude."

A series of cases involving multimember legislative districts (districts that each elected more than one member of a legislative body) or at-large elections, though not strictly speaking gerrymandering cases, shed light on how gerrymandering cases alleging violation of the Equal Protection Clause are handled. First, compare two cases involving multimember legislative districts. In both, the allegation was that a multimember district was being used to discriminate against a protected minority by effectively diluting their voting strength. In neither case was there a violation of one-person, one-vote. In the case of Indiana, it was the black residents of Indianapolis (*Whitcomb v. Chavis*, decided in 1971). In the case of Texas, it was the black residents of Dallas County and the Mexican American residents of Bexar County (San Antonio) (*White v. Register*, decided in 1973). The claim in Indiana failed, and the claim in Texas succeeded. In both cases, the district court found in favor of the plaintiffs, but the Indiana decision was reversed by the Supreme Court, and the Texas one was affirmed. How are they different? The district court's findings of fact tell the story.

In the Indiana case, the Supreme Court said that multimember districts are not "inherently invidious and violative of the Fourteenth Amendment" (*Whitcomb v. Chavis*, 160). And its review of the district court's findings of fact did not demonstrate that the use of a multimember district in this situation was "invidious." In the Supreme Court's view, the facts as found by the district court did no more than make an argument for proportional representation of an identified group. The missing ingredient was a discriminatory purpose.

In *White*, the district court had found that the black community in Dallas County and the Mexican American community in Bexar County (San Antonio) were "generally not permitted to enter into the political process in a reliable and meaningful manner," relying in part on the "history of official discrimination in Texas" for black residents of Dallas County (*White*, 767, 766). The district court concluded that Bexar County's Mexican Americans were "effectively removed from the political processes" (*White*, 769). The district court described the Mexican American community as facing cultural and language barriers that impeded participation in the political process. It found that a "cultural incompatibility . . . conjoined with the poll tax and the most restrictive voter registration procedures in the nation have operated to effectively deny Mexican-Americans access to the political processes in Texas even longer than the blacks were formally denied access by the white primary" (*White*, 768). The Supreme Court unanimously stated that on the record of this case, there was no reason to overturn the findings of the district court.

A third case involved a challenge to a county government in Georgia. The county was very large geographically, about two-thirds the size of Rhode Island, and was governed by a county commission elected by at-large countywide voting. The county had a population in 1980 of 19,349, of whom 53.6 percent were black. The plaintiffs alleged that the at-large voting was being used as a device to maintain white control of the county by diluting the strength of black voters, in violation of the Equal Protection Clause. The district court found that the at-large scheme of electing commissioners "although racially neutral when adopted is being *maintained* for invidious purposes" (*Rogers v. Lodge*, 622; decided in 1982; emphasis in original). The Supreme Court concluded that the district court had found purposeful racial discrimination and that its findings were not clearly erroneous. The district court finding was based on, among other things, the past discriminatory acts of Georgia and concluded as a factual matter, in the words of the Supreme Court, that "historical discrimination had restricted the present opportunity of blacks to effectively participate in the political process" (*Rogers*, 625).

These three cases, and especially the *Rogers v. Lodge* opinion, clarify the thinking of the Supreme Court. *Rogers* sets out the standard for violation of the Equal Protection Clause as follows: The plaintiffs must be able to prove that the alleged discriminatory law is traced to a racially discriminatory purpose or intent. It is not enough that one race be affected to a greater extent than another race. At the same time, discriminatory purpose need not be proved by direct evidence. In the *Rogers* case, the Supreme Court went on to clarify its approach to the factual findings of the district court by refusing to overturn district court findings unless they could be shown to be "clearly erroneous" (*Rogers*, 627). The net result is that if the district court finds discriminatory racial purpose or intent, and the finding is not clearly erroneous, a district court decision that the Equal Protection Clause was violated will be upheld by the Supreme Court. All three of these cases involved racial groups and were reviewed under the Supreme Court's strict scrutiny standard.

While these cases inform about the treatment of situations involving an allegation of a violation of the Equal Protection Clause as discriminating against one of the classifications explicitly recognized by the Supreme Court as calling for heightened scrutiny, they do not address cases arising under many of the claims of gerrymandering, which involve partisanship. However, the Supreme Court's requirement of a discriminatory purpose or intent as well as an actual discriminatory effect applies to the gerrymandering claims.

Justice Stevens, in casting the deciding vote in *Karcher v. Daggett* (1983), addressed the applicability of the Equal Protection Clause to gerrymandering in his concurring opinion. He stated,

> The Equal Protection Clause requires every State to govern impartially. When a State adopts rules governing its election machinery or defining electoral boundaries, those rules must serve the interests of the entire community. If they serve no purpose other than to favor one segment—whether racial, ethnic, religious, economic, or political—that may occupy a position of strength at a particular point in time, or to disadvantage a politically weak segment of the community, they violate the constitutional guarantee of equal protection." (*Karcher v. Daggett*, 748, citation omitted)

Although the usual usage of "gerrymandering" refers to political partisanship where one party seeks an advantage over another one by the arrangement of districts in the division of a territory into separate nonoverlapping districts, conceptually the group to be benefited or harmed by gerrymandering need not be a political party. It could be groups classified by income, occupation, family status, or just about any of the myriad characteristics that modern data collection and processing makes available for distinguishing between groups of people. Placing the word *partisan* in front of it should not change the analysis. Challenges to these types of classifications based on a violation of equal protection would be reviewed under the Supreme Court's rational relationship test unless it is a classification that triggers heightened scrutiny where the governmental interest must be compelling.

Partisan gerrymandering reached the Supreme Court in 1986 with *Davis v. Bandemer*. Plaintiffs claimed that Indiana's redistricting of its legislature based on the 1980 Census was designed to disadvantage

Democrats. The districting plan involved multimember districts, especially in and around Indianapolis, allegedly designed to neutralize the Democratic vote of the city. There was no basis for a claim under one person, one vote, as the population deviation between districts was no more than 1.15 percent. Following the outline contained in Justice Stevens's concurring opinion in *Karcher v. Daggett* (*Bandemer v. Davis*, 1490), the district court found that the districting plan violated the Equal Protection Clause. The Supreme Court held in a 6–3 decision that the controversy was justiciable but that the district court "had applied an insufficiently demanding standard in finding unconstitutional vote dilution" (*Davis*, 113). The Supreme Court applied the six-factor justiciability analysis set forth in *Baker v. Carr*. Only one of these factors was at issue in *Davis v. Bandemer*, the "lack of judicially discoverable and manageable standards for resolving" the matter. The Court stated that "we are not persuaded that there are no judicially discernible and manageable standards by which political gerrymander cases are to be decided" (*Davis*, 123).

As for the district court's standard, the Supreme Court found that it amounted to requiring proportional representation across party lines. The Supreme Court rejected "the District Court's apparent finding that any interference with an opportunity to elect a representative of one's choice would be sufficient to allege or make out an equal protection violation, unless justified by some acceptable state interest" (*Davis v. Bandemer*, 133; emphasis in original). Rather, "where unconstitutional vote dilution is alleged in . . . political gerrymandering, the mere lack of proportional representation alone does not constitute impermissible discrimination under the Equal Protection Clause" (*Davis v. Bandemer*, 132).

As to what the standard should be for a violation of equal protection in partisan gerrymandering cases, the majority in *Davis v. Bandemer* could not agree. Four justices agreed that "plaintiffs were required to prove both intentional discrimination against an identifiable political group and an actual discriminatory effect on that group" (*Davis*, 127). They went on to state that "[a]s long as redistricting is done by a legislature, it should not be very difficult to prove that the likely political consequences of the reapportionment were intended" (*Davis*, 129). They concluded that the record in this case supported a finding that the discrimination against the Democrats was intentional. This plurality of justices concluded, properly, that the simple fact that an apportionment scheme makes elections more difficult to win or that there is a "mere lack of proportional representation will not be sufficient to prove unconstitutional discrimination" (*Davis*, 132). This is where the plurality went astray by adopting the following approach: "[U]nconstitutional discrimination occurs only when the electoral system is arranged in a manner that will consistently degrade a voter's or a group of voters' influence on the political process as a whole" (*Davis*, 132). It was unnecessary to go beyond their determination of the inadequacy of proportional representation, since in this case that was the principal offer of proof. As will be seen, the plurality's approach has not been a successful solution. A major problem with the plurality's standard is that its evidentiary requirements are so difficult to meet that it amounts to no meaningful test at all, even in the face of unquestionable partisan discrimination involving bizarrely shaped and distorted districts. (See the various opinions in *Vieth v. Jubelirer* for general agreement that the plurality's standard did not work.)

When reading the case, one is struck by how much the writing is slanted by the fact that, in the case, the claimed discrimination is partisan—that is, focused on political parties—when other groups could also be discriminated against in gerrymandering activity. Determination of the discriminatory intent and effect of alleged gerrymandering must involve analysis of partisan outcomes under proposed or actual redistricting plans being challenged because the allegation is that the activity aims to affect elections and the votes of citizens. But once these hurdles are met, the focus should shift in search of a remedy. And the remedy should seek to eliminate the technique used to implement the unconstitutional action, namely the distortion of district boundaries. Once discrimination against a group is shown, inquire about the limits of acceptable gerrymandering. Justice Powell in his dissent in *Davis* (joined by Justice Stevens) did touch on this when he focused on "whether the boundaries of the voting districts have been distorted deliberately and arbitrarily to achieve illegitimate ends" (*Davis*, 165).

Gerrymandering is achieved by introducing district boundaries that frequently take obscure paths and often appear as shapes bearing no rational relationship to common sense principles of dividing up a geographical area into nonoverlapping subdistricts with no discontinuities within each subdistrict. After all, it is the geographical distortion of district boundaries that offends one's sense of fairness. These have been variously described in Supreme Court cases as "a strangely irregular twenty-eight-sided figure" (Justice Frankfurter in *Gomillion v. Lightfoot*, 341); "deliberate and arbitrary distortion of district boundaries and populations for partisan or personal political purposes" (Justice Fortas in *Kirkpatrick*, 537); "grotesquely gerrymandered" (Justice Powell in *Davis v. Bandemer*, 162); "among those well-settled principles is the understanding that a district's peculiar shape might be a symptom of an illicit purpose in the line-drawing process" (Justice Stevens in *Vieth v. Jubelirer*, 321); and "having ignored reasonable alternatives consistent" with geographical contiguity and compactness (Justice Souter in *Vieth v. Jubelirer*, 348, 351).

The change in the capacity to discern differences in the proclivities of voters in ever-smaller geographical areas and to utilize them in constructing legislative districts jeopardizes the fundamental concept of a democracy of the people. Three of the justices in *Vieth v. Jubelirer*, a case challenging the congressional districts in Pennsylvania, recognized this threat. Justice Kennedy viewed the evolution of technology and computer-assisted districting as a threat if the courts do not hear claims of partisan gerrymandering. It is also true that Justice Kennedy had a hope that technology might also facilitate the hearing and resolution of partisan gerrymandering claims (*Vieth*, 312). Justice Souter stated that "the increasing efficiency of partisan redistricting has damaged the democratic process" (*Vieth*, 345). Justice Breyer also expressed concern about developing technology. He stated that "[t]he availability of enhanced computer technology allows the parties to redraw boundaries in ways that target individual neighborhoods and homes, carving out safe but slim victory margins in the maximum number of districts, with little risk of cutting their margins too thin" (*Vieth*, 364).

The Supreme Court revisited partisan gerrymandering in 2004. The case, *Vieth v. Jubelirer*, involved a claim of partisan gerrymandering of congressional districts in Pennsylvania following the 2000 Census; the complaint described the districts as "meandering and irregular" and said they "ignor[ed] all traditional redistricting criteria, including the preservation of local government boundaries, solely for the sake of partisan advantage" (quoted in *Vieth v. Jubelirer*, 272–73). The district court dismissed the partisan gerrymandering claim, finding that the plaintiffs had not met the standard set forth by the plurality in *Davis v. Bandemer* (*Vieth v. Pennsylvania*, 543–47). The Supreme Court affirmed with no agreement by a majority of the Court on the grounds for affirmation. Four justices (Scalia, Rehnquist, O'Connor, and Thomas) voted to affirm because they wanted to overrule *Davis* on the question of justiciability, and one justice (Kennedy) voted to affirm but contended that the case was justiciable. And four other justices (Stevens, Souter, Breyer, and Ginsberg) voted to uphold *Davis*, finding the matter to be justiciable.

Furthermore, as in *Davis*, the majority of the Court finding that partisan gerrymandering was justiciable could not agree on any standard for resolving the matter. Justice Stevens proposed the following test:

> [A]sk whether the legislature allowed partisan considerations to dominate and control the lines drawn, forsaking all neutral principles. Under my analysis, if no neutral criteria can be identified to justify the lines drawn, and if the only possible explanation for a district's bizarre shape is a naked desire to increase partisan strength, then no rational basis exists to save the district from an equal protection challenge. (*Vieth v. Jubelirer*, 339)

Justice Souter's suggested test is quite similar to Justice Stevens's. (Justice Ginsberg joined Justice Souter in his dissent.) Justice Souter would require that a "district paid little or no heed to those traditional districting principles whose disregard can be shown straightforwardly: contiguity, compactness, disregard for political subdivisions such as municipal boundaries, and conformity with geographic features like rivers and mountains" (*Vieth v. Jubelirer*, 348). Justice Breyer's suggestion is less helpful, focusing on "unjustified use of political factors to entrench a minority in power" (*Vieth v. Jubelirer*, 360; emphasis in original).

Justice Kennedy offers no suggested standard but holds out hope for one. In his opinion, he seems to want a standard that "promises political neutrality." He states in commenting on a criterion that "we could not assure . . . that this criterion, neutral enough on its face, would not in fact benefit one political party over another" (*Vieth v. Jubelirer*, 309). But that is not the point. The point is not to assure political neutrality; it is to remove abusive practices. Any standard will still leave some participants with an advantage. After all, that is what the rejection of proportional districting (drawing districts so that the expected outcome of district elections reflects each political party's proportion of the statewide vote) is all about. Even the one-person, one-vote standard permits partisan outcomes. But it limits the latitude for action. That is all that needs to be done when it comes to gerrymandering.

Justice Scalia's opinion was written as an opinion reversing the decision in *Davis v. Bandemer,* even though that did not happen. Among other matters, it addressed the history of political gerrymandering as supporting a conclusion that the matter should be found to be nonjusticiable. He argued that political gerrymandering was "alive and well (though not yet known by that name) at the time of the framing" (Vieth, 274). But this reasoning lacks any convincing force and flies in the face of the facts applicable to the population disparity and to the gerrymandering situations.

A comparison to the same argument that could have been made with respect to the one-person, one-vote cases shows the weakness of Justice Scalia's argument. Following the 1800 Census, nine states elected their members of the US House of Representatives from congressional districts. Seven states elected their members of the House of Representatives in statewide at-large elections. At that time, the Constitution required that slaves be counted as three-fifths of a person for apportionment purposes. As a result, the census population figures for the number of persons have been adjusted to reflect this requirement in constructing comparisons across congressional districts in states for the Eighth Congress. The distribution of adjusted population across congressional districts in each of the states electing them from districts is summarized in Table 1, which is taken from Appendix A. Table 1 also compares these 1800 districts to the population variations that were rejected as not complying with the one-person, one-vote rule applicable to congressional districting in *Karcher v. Daggett.*

Table 1 shows that each of the various states using congressional districts to elect their representatives had districts that varied widely from the concept that within each state the adjusted population of each congressional district should be close to equal. The adjusted population difference between the largest- and smallest-populated districts as a percentage of the mathematical ideal of equality for a state varied between 21 percent and 53 percent. And the ratio of the largest- to the smallest-populated district in a state varied from 1.24 to 1.66. These differences from population equality across districts in each of these states violated the one-person, one-vote rule in all cases. In *Karcher v. Daggett,* a districting plan for congressional districts in New Jersey was found to be

Table 1   Summary of Adjusted Population Characteristics of Congressional Districts for the Eighth Congress (1803–1805) and Rejected Districts in *Karcher v. Daggett.*

State	Adjusted Population of Smallest District	Adjusted Population of Largest District	Difference as a Percent of Ideal Adjusted Population*	Ratio of Largest- to Smallest-Populated District
Kentucky	29,583	38,608	26	1.31
Maryland	27,581	43,516	48	1.58
Massachusetts	28,135	45,390	51	1.61
New York	28,897	47,131	53	1.63
North Carolina	31,649	39,170	21	1.24
Pennsylvania	28,264	38,738	31	1.37
South Carolina	30,090	40,702	30	1.35
Vermont	30,533	50,525	52	1.65
Virginia	25,438	42,327	50	1.66
Districts rejected in *Karcher v. Daggett*	523,798	527,472	0.7	1.01

Source: See Appendix A.
* The difference is the population of the largest district in terms of population minus that of the smallest one. The ideal population is the state's population divided by the number of representatives it has in the US House of Representatives.

in noncompliance with a population difference between the largest- and smallest-populated districts as a percentage of the mathematical ideal of equality of 0.70 and a ratio of the largest- to the smallest-populated district equal to 1.01.

This early history only shows that at the beginning of the United States, the various legislatures imperfectly expressed fairness and an understanding of "by the people" and does not mean that the framers intended that this imperfection should become the standard. There is ample evidence that the framers intended that members of the House of Representatives be elected by people with equally weighted votes. The election of the House of Representatives by the people was half of the Great Compromise that made the present Constitution possible, the other half being the election of the Senate by the state legislatures. At the Constitutional Convention, the meaning of election by the people was expressed by numerous delegates in terms similar to those used by James Wilson of Pennsylvania that "equal numbers of people ought to have an equal no. of representatives" and that representatives "of different districts ought clearly to hold the same proportion to each other, as their respective constituents hold to each other" (quoted from *Wesberry v. Sanders*, 11; see also *Wesberry v. Sanders*, 7–18, on the historical record, and Hacker, 6–14). The one-person, one-vote standard is both egalitarian and responsive to the rights of individual citizens. It has been widely accepted and forms the basis for many analyses of qualitative vote dilution such as gerrymandering. And if Justice Scalia's misreading of history were followed, it would not be the law of the land today. Of even greater importance is the fact that the Equal Protection Clause applies to the formation of congressional districts as well as state legislative districts, and it was adopted in 1868. It clearly is not limited by what was taking place at the time of the framing of the Constitution or at the time of its adoption. Its purpose was to change things, not to codify them.

Just as it did not make sense to look at the population distribution of congressional districts at the outset of the United States when interpreting the meaning of "by the people" in the malapportionment cases, it makes no more sense to look at whether gerrymandering existed as a concept at the inception of the country. And we certainly should not give much credence to the man after whom this practice is named, Elbridge Gerry, who advocated limiting the representatives from new western states so that they would never exceed in total those of the original thirteen. The maps of the congressional districts represented in Table 1 are included in Appendix A. A perusal of these maps indicates little of the type of gerrymandering that people find objectionable today. Compare them with the gerrymandering depicted in Figure 4 from *Gomillion v. Lightfoot* and the districts that the Supreme Court of Pennsylvania found in a February 2018 decision to violate the state constitution, shown in Figure 5.

The Pennsylvania Supreme Court described the so-called 2011 Plan shown in Figure 5 in this way: "[A] lay examination of the Plan . . . reveals tortuously drawn districts that cause plainly unnecessary political-subdivision splits" (*League of Women Voters v. Commonwealth*

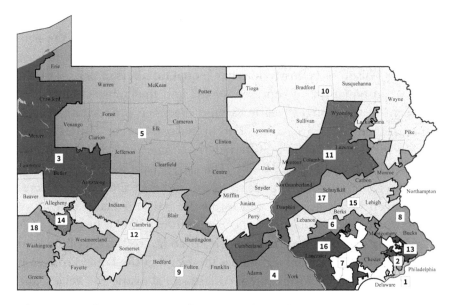

Figure 5 The Congressional Districts from the Pennsylvania Congressional Redistricting Act of 2011.

Source: Per Curium Opinion and Order in *League of Women Voters of Pennsylvania v. Commonwealth of Pennsylvania* Ordering a Remedial Plan, dated February 19, 2018.

of Pennsylvania, Opinion, 127). That court went on to expand on its description of the 2011 Plan as follows:

> In terms of compactness, a rudimentary review reveals a map comprised of oddly shaped, sprawling districts which wander seemingly arbitrarily across Pennsylvania, leaving 28 counties, 68 political subdivisions, and numerous wards, divided among as many as five congressional districts, in their wakes. Significantly, these districts often rend municipalities from their surrounding metropolitan areas and quizzically divide small municipalities which could easily be incorporated into single districts without detriment to the traditional redistricting criteria. . . . [T]he 7th Congressional District, pictured above, has been referred to as resembling "Goofy kicking Donald Duck," and is perhaps chief among a number of rivals in this regard, ambling from Philadelphia's suburbs in central Montgomery County, where it borders four other districts, south into Delaware County, where it abuts a fifth, then west into

Chester County, where it abuts another district and travels north-west before jutting out in both northerly and southerly directions into Berks and Lancaster Counties. Indeed, it is difficult to imagine how a district as Rorschachian and sprawling, which is contiguous in two locations only by virtue of a medical facility and a seafood/steakhouse, respectively, might plausibly be referred to as "compact." Moreover, in terms of political subdivision splits, the 7th Congressional District splits each of the five counties in its path and some 26 separate political subdivisions between multiple congressional districts. . . . The 7th Congressional District, however, is merely the starkest example of the 2011 Plan's overall composition. . . . [T]he 2011 Plan's congressional districts similarly sprawl through Pennsylvania's landscape, often contain "isthmuses" and "tentacles," and almost entirely ignore the integrity of political subdivisions in their trajectories. (*League of Women Voters v. Commonwealth of Pennsylvania*, Opinion, 127–28)

The 2011 Plan rejected by the Pennsylvania Supreme Court is an excellent illustration of what is wrong with the modern-day implementation of gerrymandering. As in the case of one-person, one-vote, where in the initial case the difference between the largest- and the smallest-populated congressional districts as a percentage of the mathematical ideal was 140 percent, and the ratio of the largest- to the smallest-populated congressional district was 3.03 (*Wesberry v. Sanders*, 2), no one contemplated the creation of congressional districts with the tortuous and odd shapes depicted in Figure 5.

It is a straightforward process to show, using statistical methods, that the layperson's impression that a district map like Figure 5 is drawn without regard to any conception of compactness is correct. Such evidence was a part of the Pennsylvania case. Among the statistical measures were the Reock Compactness Score and the Polsby-Popper Compactness Score (Reock; Polsby and Popper). The Reock Compactness Score is the ratio of a district's area to the area of the smallest circle that can be drawn to enclose the district. The Polsby-Popper Compactness Score is the ratio of the district's area to the area of a circle whose circumference equals the district's perimeter. Each of these has values ranging from 0 to 1, with 1 being the most compact and 0 the least compact. Of course, in the real world the extremities of the range of values are not the actual lower and upper bounds, as a state cannot have districts of no area (value of zero) or districts that are all circles (value of one).

What distinguishes the case involving the districting plan in Figure 5 is that it is a state court case decided entirely under principles of state law and not relying to any extent on federal law. Thus, the US Supreme Court refused to hear the case when the defendants tried to appeal the decision of the Pennsylvania Supreme Court to it. How had the Pennsylvania Supreme Court arrived at its decision?

The Pennsylvania Constitution contains a provision that the Pennsylvania Supreme Court referred to as the "Free and Equal Elections Clause." This clause provides:

> Elections shall be free and equal; and no power, civil or military, shall at any time interfere to prevent the free exercise of the right of suffrage." (Pa. Const. art. I, § 5; *League of Women Voters v. Commonwealth of Pennsylvania*, Opinion, 100)

In commenting on this clause, the Pennsylvania Supreme Court stated as follows:

> In accordance with the plain and expansive sweep of the words "free and equal," we view them as indicative of the framers' intent that all aspects of the electoral process, to the greatest degree possible, be kept open and unrestricted to the voters of our Commonwealth, and, also, conducted in a manner which guarantees, to the greatest degree possible, a voter's right to equal participation in the electoral process for the selection of his or her representatives in government. . . . (*League of Women Voters v. Commonwealth of Pennsylvania*, Opinion, 100)
>
> [T]he consequences of a particular interpretation are also relevant in our analysis. Specifically, partisan gerrymandering dilutes the votes of those who in prior elections voted for the party not in power to give the party in power a lasting electoral advantage. By placing voters preferring one party's candidates in districts where their votes are wasted on candidates likely to lose (cracking), or by placing such voters in districts where their votes are cast for candidates destined to win (packing), the non-favored party's votes are diluted. It is axiomatic that a diluted vote is not an equal vote, as

all voters do not have an equal opportunity to translate their votes into representation. This is the antithesis of a healthy representative democracy. Indeed, for our form of government to operate as intended, each and every Pennsylvania voter must have the same free and equal *opportunity* to select his or her representatives. . . . Furthermore, adoption of a broad interpretation guards against the risk of unfairly rendering votes nugatory, artificially entrenching representative power, and discouraging voters from participating in the electoral process because they have come to believe that the power of their individual vote has been diminished to the point that it "does not count." A broad and robust interpretation of Article I, Section 5 [the Free and Equal Elections Clause], serves as a bulwark against the adverse consequences of partisan gerrymandering. (*League of Women Voters v. Commonwealth of Pennsylvania*, Opinion, 118; emphasis in original)

Then the Pennsylvania Supreme Court turned to the question of "what measures should be utilized to assess a dilution claim under the Free and Equal Elections Clause" (*League of Women Voters v. Commonwealth of Pennsylvania*, Opinion, 120). The Pennsylvania Supreme Court concluded that the measure of whether a congressional district plan complies with the Free and Equal Elections Clause is whether the districts are

composed of compact and contiguous territory; as nearly equal in population as practicable; and which do not divide any county, city, incorporated town, borough, township, or ward, except where necessary to ensure equality of population. (*League of Women Voters v. Commonwealth of Pennsylvania*, Opinion, 123)

All other factors taken into account in the districting process are viewed as subordinate to the neutral criteria of contiguity, compactness, minimization of the division of political subdivisions, and population equality. If these neutral factors are subordinated "in whole or in part to extraneous considerations such as gerrymandering for unfair political advantage," the Free and Equal Elections Clause of the Pennsylvania Constitution is violated (*League of Women Voters v. Commonwealth of Pennsylvania*, Opinion, 123). This result was aided by, but not solely based on, a provision contained in the Pennsylvania Constitution that requires State Senate and representative districts to "be composed of compact and contiguous territory as nearly equal in population as practicable" (Pa. Const. Art. 2, §16; *League of Women Voters v. Commonwealth of Pennsylvania*, Opinion, 121).

Furthermore, the Pennsylvania Supreme Court notes that under Pennsylvania law "this standard *does not require* a showing that the creators of congressional districts *intentionally* subordinated these traditional criteria to other considerations in the creation of the district in order for it to violate Article I, Section 5 [the Free and Equal Elections Clause]; rather, it is sufficient to establish a violation of this section to show that these traditional criteria were subordinated to other factors" (*League of Women Voters v. Commonwealth of Pennsylvania*, Opinion, 124; emphasis added). In comparison, the US Supreme Court has a requirement of intentional discrimination. It is interesting to note that *Vieth v. Jubelirer* involved another Pennsylvania districting plan that was nearly as offensive as the one in *League of Women Voters v. Commonwealth of Pennsylvania*. (See *Vieth v. Jubelirer*, Appendix to Opinion of Justice Stevens, for a copy of that plan.)

The Pennsylvania Supreme Court had no problem concluding that the proposed 2011 districting plan failed to pass muster. It found that the evidence "demonstrates that the Plan cannot plausibly be directed at drawing equally populous, compact, and contiguous districts which divide political subdivisions only as necessary to ensure equal population" (*League of Women Voters v. Commonwealth of Pennsylvania*, Opinion, 124).

One part of the evidence dramatically demonstrates the distance of the state's plan from acceptability. An expert witness (Dr. Jowei Chen) used computer algorithms to create two random sets of 500 simulated alternative districting plans for Pennsylvania's congressional districts. The first set "utilized traditional Pennsylvania districting criteria, specifically: population equality, contiguity, compactness, absence of splits within municipalities, unless necessary, and absence of splits within counties, unless necessary" (*League of Women Voters v. Commonwealth of Pennsylvania*, Opinion, 40). The second set of 500 simulated alternative districting plans used the same criteria as the first set plus the criterion of protecting incumbents.

The sets of simulated plans were compared with the state's plan (Act 131). The comparison on the criteria of compactness is especially

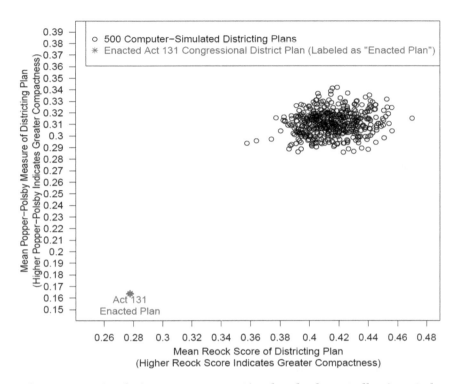

Figure 6 Simulation Set 1: 500 Simulated Plans Following Only Traditional Districting Criteria (No Consideration of Incumbent Protection).

Source: "Expert Report of Jowei Chen, PhD," in *League of Women Voters v. Commonwealth of Pennsylvania*, Opinion.

informative. Figures 6 and 7 show two measures of compactness: the average of the Reock Compactness Score for the districts in each simulated plan or for the state plan is on the horizontal axis, and the average of the Polsby-Popper Compactness Score for the districts in each simulated plan or for the state plan is on the vertical axis. Figure 6 is for the first set of simulations; Figure 7 is for the second set of simulations. Some care needs to be exercised in comparing the two figures because the scale is different in them. Two observations are clearly evident. The first is that protecting incumbents (Figure 7) results in outcomes that are below and to the left of the scattergram without incumbency protection (Figure 6), and hence not acceptable in the absence of incumbency protection. This is not surprising because the incumbents were elected from districts that are the subject of challenge in the case before the

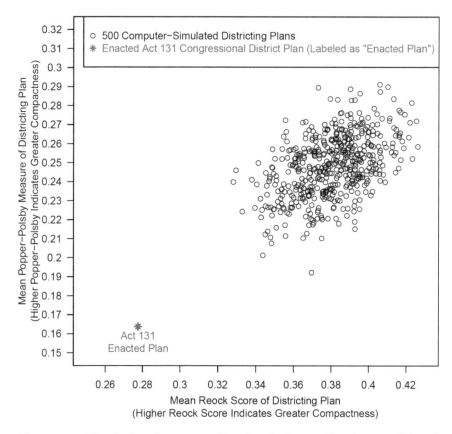

Figure 7   Simulation Set 2: 500 Simulated Plans Following Traditional Districting Criteria and Protecting Seventeen Incumbents.

Source: "Expert Report of Jowei Chen, PhD," in *League of Women Voters v. Commonwealth of Pennsylvania.*

Pennsylvania court. Second, in both figures, the state's plan—Act 131— is in the lower far-left-hand corner, representing a result with close to no compactness, while all the simulated plans are in the upper right-hand corner, representing a high degree of compactness. The state's plan clearly fails any compactness assessment miserably.

The Pennsylvania Supreme Court gave the state legislature and governor an opportunity to enact a complying districting plan but stated that if they did not do so by a specified date, the Court would implement one. The state legislature and governor did not enact an alternative plan, and the court ordered the implementation of a remedial plan that it developed. This plan is shown in Figure 8. It is easy to see

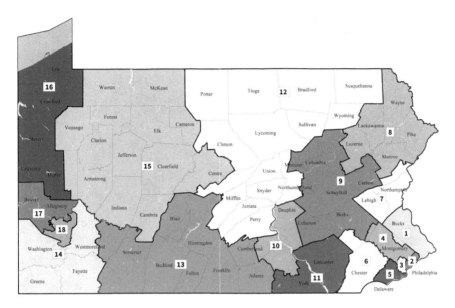

Figure 8 Remedial Plan Adopted by the Pennsylvania Supreme Court in *League of Women Voters of Pennsylvania v. Commonwealth of Pennsylvania*.

Source: *League of Women Voters of Pennsylvania v. Commonwealth of Pennsylvania* (Remedy on February 19, 2018), Appendix A.

the improvement by comparing it with Figure 5. According to the compactness report referenced in the Pennsylvania Supreme Court's remedial order, its remedial plan had a Reock Compactness Score average (across the congressional districts) value of 0.46 and a Polsby-Popper Compactness Score average value of 0.33, which is a point within the scattergram area of Figure 6 and above and to the right of the scattergram in Figure 7, also an acceptable area.

As of June 2019, thirteen states (including Pennsylvania) had a clause in their state constitutions that was the same as the Pennsylvania Free and Equal Elections Clause, and an additional twelve states had a clause requiring elections to be free, for a total of twenty-five states. The constitutions of twenty-five states had a requirement to use compactness in districting of the state legislature or of congressional districts. And thirty-eight states had at least one of these three requirements in their constitutions. The constitutions of thirty-eight states had a requirement to use contiguous territory, and forty had a requirement that the

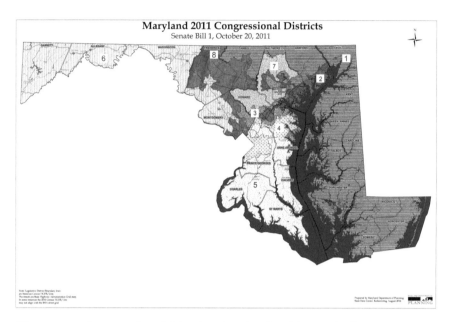

Figure 9   Congressional Districts in Maryland in *Benisek v. Lamone.*

populations of districts be as equal as practicable. Only three states (Iowa, Kansas, and South Carolina) had no requirement with respect to any of these matters. (See Appendix B.)

In 2018, the US Supreme Court considered partisan gerrymandering claims in two cases but managed to dispose of both of them on procedural grounds. In *Gill v. Whitford,* involving Wisconsin state legislative districts, the Court decided that standing was lacking and remanded for the plaintiffs to submit additional evidence on standing. In *Benisek v. Lamone,* involving Maryland congressional districts, the issue was whether a district court's denial of a preliminary injunction was proper, which denial the Supreme Court upheld.

In March 2019, the US Supreme Court heard arguments in two partisan gerrymandering cases. One of these cases is the sequel to *Benisek,* decided in 2018 on procedural grounds, which now arrived at the Supreme Court with a three-judge district court decision on the merits. The Maryland congressional districts under review in *Benisek v. Lamone* are shown in Figure 9. The plaintiffs claimed that the state's approved redistricting plan discriminated against Republicans.

The district court decision in *Benisek v. Lamone* is based on finding that the changes made to the Maryland Sixth Congressional District violated the plaintiffs' First Amendment rights, an approach suggested by Justice Kennedy in his concurrence in *Vieth v. Jubelirer*. The district court reasoned as follows:

> To be sure, citizens have no constitutional right to be assigned to a district that is likely to elect a representative that shares their views. But they do have a right under the First Amendment not to have the value of their vote diminished *because of* the political views they have expressed through their party affiliation and voting history. Put simply, partisan vote dilution, when intentionally imposed, involves the State penalizing voters for expressing a viewpoint while, at the same time, rewarding voters for expressing the opposite viewpoint. (*Benisek v. Lamone* District Court on Merits, 15; emphasis in the original)

The Supreme Court had not directly addressed the question of whether partisan gerrymandering violates the First Amendment. A plurality of four justices in *Vieth v. Jubelirer* suggested that the First Amendment was inappropriate for gerrymandering cases when they stated that

> a First Amendment claim, if it were sustained, would render unlawful *all* consideration of political affiliation in districting, just as it renders unlawful *all* consideration of political affiliation in hiring for non-policy-level government jobs. (*Vieth v. Jubelirer*, 294; emphasis in the original)

The plurality seemed to think it obvious that such a result was undesirable, maybe even absurd. But is it? The framers of the Constitution were fearful of political parties. Hamilton and Madison in *Federalist Papers* Nos. 9 and 10 addressed the destructive role of factions. It was stated in *Federalist Paper* No. 10 that "[n]o man is allowed to be a judge in his own cause, because his interest would certainly bias his judgment. . . . With equal, nay with greater reason, a body of men are unfit to be both judges and parties at the same time." This seems more like a sentiment that partisanship should be limited in district formation, not one that it should be given its free rein. And George Washington, the first president, did not belong to a political party, and in his farewell address he warned his countrymen of the dangers of political parties, "with

particular reference to the founding of them on geographical discrim-
inations." More broadly addressing political party dangers, Washington
advised that "the common and continual mischiefs of the spirit of party
are sufficient to make it the interest and duty of a wise people to dis-
courage and restrain it."

The Supreme Court has acknowledged that partisan interests are
inherent in the apportionment process. As it stated in *Gaffney v. Cummings,*

> It is not only obvious, but absolutely unavoidable, that the location
> and shape of districts may well determine the political complexion
> of the area. District lines are rarely neutral phenomena. They can
> well determine what district will be predominantly Democratic or
> predominantly Republican, or make a close race likely. Redistrict-
> ing may pit incumbents against one another or make very difficult
> the election of the most experienced legislator. The reality is that
> districting inevitably has and is intended to have substantial politi-
> cal consequences." (*Gaffney v. Cummings,* 753)

This does not mean that limits cannot be placed on the abusive use of
district boundary definition to achieve partisan gains. It only means that
whatever standard is used will leave a residual where partisanship may
play a legitimate role. The abuse is not partisanship per se, but the distortion of district boundaries for partisan gain. And that can be remedied.

The approach taken by the state court in the Pennsylvania case
might have been a preferable way to address the allegations presented
in the Maryland case. It is interesting to note that the Maryland Constitution requires the use of contiguity, compactness, population equality,
regard for natural boundaries, and regard for the boundaries of political units in redistricting of the state legislature while being silent on
congressional redistricting. The First Amendment approach does not
seem to offer a way to determine when partisanship is too much. The
Pennsylvania court's approach does.

The other case before the Supreme Court in March 2019 involved
a three-judge district court finding that the 2016 congressional districts
of North Carolina were gerrymandered in violation of the Equal Protection Clause, the First Amendment, and Article I of the US Constitution (*Common Cause v. Rucho*). The proposed congressional districts
under review in *Common Cause v. Rucho* are shown in Figure 10. The

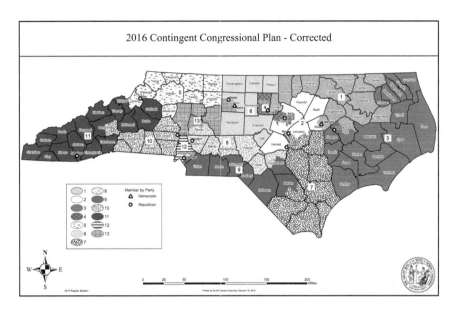

Figure 10 Proposed Congressional Districts for North Carolina in *Common Cause v. Rucho.*

plaintiffs claimed that the state's approved redistricting plan discriminated against Democrats.

In light of *Vieth v. Jubelirer,* what standard did the district court apply under the plaintiffs' claim that the North Carolina districting plan violated the Equal Protection Clause? The district court found "a predominant intent to subordinate the interests of non-Republican voters and entrench Republican control of North Carolina's congressional delegation" and that the state's adopted plan had this effect (*Common Cause v. Rucho,* 205). The district court also found that the state's districting plan violated the First Amendment because it "intended to disfavor supporters of non-Republican candidates based on those supporters' past expressions of political beliefs," it "burdened such supporters' political speech and associational rights," and "a causal relationship exists between . . . [the state's] discriminatory motivation and the First Amendment burden imposed by" the state's districting plan (*Common Cause v. Rucho,* 275–76). The district court also found that the state's plan was "not authorized by the Elections Clause" in Article I of the Constitution (*Common Cause v. Rucho,* 288).

What was the evidence that the district court relied on in the North Carolina case? Among other things, it included expert testimony on alternative redistricting plans for the state. One expert (Dr. Jonathan Mattingly) drew a random sample of more than 150,000 simulated alternative plans using computer technology and ordinary statistical methods. Then, Dr. Mattingly used a computer algorithm to eliminate

> from the 150,000 plan sample all "unreasonable" districting plans—plans with noncontiguous districts, plans with population deviations exceeding 0.1 percent, plans that were not reasonably compact under common statistical measures of compactness, plans that did not minimize the number of county and VTD [census voting district] splits, and plans that did not comply with the Voting Rights Act—yielding a 24,518-plan ensemble. The criteria Dr. Mattingly used to eliminate "unreasonable" plans from his sample reflect traditional redistricting criteria, . . . [*Harris v. Arizona Independent Redistricting Commission*, 136 S. Ct. at 1306 (recognizing compactness, contiguity, maintaining integrity of political subdivisions, and, potentially, compliance with the Voting Rights Act, as "legitimate" considerations for deviations from population equality in state redistricting plans)], and nearly all non-partisan criteria adopted by the North Carolina legislature's Joint Select Committee on Congressional Redistricting. (*Common Cause v. Rucho*, 148)

Based on the analysis of these alternative districting plans and the plan adopted by the state, Dr. Mattingly concluded that the state's plan was an extremely unusual outcome, as only 0.7 percent of the simulated plans produced similar outcomes. In other words, 24,396 simulated plans produced outcomes more compatible with neutral districting criteria (i.e., criteria that did not use any information about the characteristics of persons other than their place of residence) than the state plan's. Dr. Mattingly concluded that the state could not "have created a redistricting plan that yielded [the results of the state's plan] unintentionally" (*Common Cause v. Rucho*, 154).

Another expert (Dr. Jowei Chen) drew three random sets of 1,000 alternative districting plans for North Carolina's congressional districts. The most important of these is the random set of 1,000 alternative plans drawn using the following criteria: population equality, contiguity, minimizing county and VTD splits, and maximizing compactness. Another set used the same criteria plus not putting incumbents in the same district. The third set of plans used the same criteria as the first set plus matching the number of split counties and paired incumbents in the state's plan. By comparing the 1,000 alternative districting plans with the state's plan, Dr. Chen concluded that the state's plan "was an extreme partisan outlier" (*Common Cause v. Rucho*, 157).

The Supreme Court combined the Maryland and North Carolina cases into a single case when they reached it and issued its decision as *Rucho v. Common Cause* in June 2019. The Supreme Court reversed course by a narrow 5–4 vote and decided that it lacked jurisdiction because "partisan gerrymandering claims present political questions beyond the reach of the federal courts" (*Rucho v. Common Cause*, majority slip opinion, 30). In 1986, the Supreme Court by a vote of 6–3 found that these cases were justiciable. The *Rucho* majority does not directly come out and state that they are overruling *Davis*; instead, they briefly mention that a majority agreed that the cases were justiciable and went on to dwell on the lack of agreement on a standard for judicial review. The *Rucho* majority gave great weight to the opinion of a plurality in *Vieth v. Jubelirer* that argued for these types of cases to be found nonjusticiable as lacking a "judicially discernible and manageable standard." The plurality in *Vieth*, which was really a minority on the point of justiciability, is cited by the *Rucho* majority at least fourteen times in a bootstrap operation if there ever was one.

The first thing to clarify about the *Rucho* majority is that there is no disagreement that there is a constitutional violation. The *Rucho* majority recites the facts of the two cases and does not dispute that they involve constitutional violations. The *Rucho* majority characterizes the cases before the Court as "districting plans . . . [that] are highly partisan, by any standard" (*Rucho v. Common Cause*, majority slip opinion, 2). And again, the *Rucho* majority states that "[e]xcessive partisanship in districting leads to results that reasonably seem unjust" (*Rucho v. Common Cause*, majority slip opinion, 30). And further, the somewhat strange statement that "[o]ur conclusion does not condone excessive partisan gerrymandering" (*Rucho v. Common Cause*, majority slip opinion, 31). But after reciting the constitutional violations, the *Rucho* majority focuses on the justiciability of the cases. Justice Kagan in her dissent states that "[f]or the first time ever, this Court refuses to remedy a constitutional violation because it thinks the task beyond judicial capabilities" (*Rucho v. Common Cause*, dissent slip opinion, 2). Yet, the *Rucho* majority recommends that gerrymandering claims be resolved by state courts as if they have a greater capability than the Supreme Court. This is an acknowledgment that gerrymandering cases are subject to effective meaningful remedies, notwithstanding the majority's self-serving denial.

What was the reasoning of the *Rucho* majority? It can be organized into six categories:

1. Some types of cases and controversies should not be accepted by the federal judiciary, citing *Baker v. Carr* for the political question doctrine. The *Rucho* majority led off this argument with the claim that the Supreme Court has understood the case or controversy "limitation to mean that federal courts can address only questions 'historically viewed as capable of resolution through the judicial process,'" quoting from a 1968 decision (*Rucho* majority slip opinion, 6–7). The statement is patently false and/or revisionist. Just examine *Colegrove v. Green*, where the Supreme Court found that it did not have jurisdiction over one-person, one-vote claims due to their being nonjusticiable, only to have this completely reversed by *Baker v. Carr*. History is not any kind of consistent guide to these issues. That *Baker v. Carr* established a more coherent description of the justiciability question does not erase history.

2. Gerrymandering existed at the time of the founding of the country. But this fails to support the *Rucho* court's conclusion because the violation of one person, one vote was even more prevalent than relatively minor gerrymandering at the time of the country's founding. See the congressional district maps from 1802 set forth at the end of Appendix A and the discussion above. Furthermore, the framers of the Constitution were concerned about partisan influence and warned of its dangers, expressing the sentiment that partisanship should be limited. And most important, the Equal Protection Clause was adopted in 1868, and whatever was happening at the framing of the Constitution or even at the time of adoption was no constraint; the Fourteenth Amendment was adopted to change the way things were being done. History was no bar to its scope or breadth.

3. The framers of the Constitution resolved the issues surrounding the election of members of the House of Representatives through the Elections Clause by having state legislatures perform districting subject to any rules adopted by the Congress (Article I). Another vacuous argument because it applies equally to one-person, one-vote cases, and not even the *Rucho* majority hints that those cases are not justiciable. Remember that Congress at one time and for a considerable period of time required equal populations in congressional districts in the same state and for some time required compact districts. The fact that Congress acted and later deleted these requirements did not deter the Supreme Court from establishing the one-person, one-vote rule. It should not have any different influence on the gerrymandering claims. And the Equal Protection Clause, adopted in 1868, applies to the actions of the state legislatures in performing their districting duties. The provisions of Article I were not exempted from the equal protection requirement. In fact, the Supreme Court has held that it also constrains the federal government.

4. The lack of "judicially discoverable and manageable standards for resolving it" (quoted from *Baker v. Carr* at *Rucho* majority slip opinion, 11) is the heart of the *Rucho* majority's reasons for concluding that partisan gerrymandering claims are not justiciable. The majority seeks to distinguish the results in the one-person, one-vote cases as follows:

> Partisan gerrymandering claims have proven far more difficult to adjudicate. The basic reason is that while it is illegal for a jurisdiction to depart from the one-person one-vote rule, or to engage in racial discrimination in districting, "a jurisdiction may engage in constitutional gerrymandering." (*Rucho* majority slip opinion, 12)

But what exactly does this statement say? First, why is it illegal for a jurisdiction to depart from the one-person, one-vote rule? Because *Baker v. Carr* decided those claims were justiciable. The same applies here. If gerrymandering claims were decided to be justiciable, then deviating from districting standards would also be illegal. Second, what is constitutional gerrymandering? This is a statement of result, not an argument for one.

5. Inability to delineate how much partisanship is too much is another category of the majority's reasoning. The *Rucho* majority are blinded by the acceptability of partisanship in elective politics. For example, they state that "[p]artisan gerrymandering claims *rest on an instinct* that groups with a certain level of political support should enjoy a commensurate level of political power and influence" (*Rucho* majority slip opinion, 16; emphasis added). And further they state that "[p]artisan gerrymandering claims invariably sound in a desire for proportional representation" (*Rucho* majority slip opinion, 16). Continuing, the majority state that "[u]nable to claim that the Constitution requires proportional representation outright, plaintiffs inevitably ask the courts to make their own political judgment about how much representation particular political parties *deserve*" (*Rucho* majority slip opinion, 17; emphasis in the original).

Partisanship refers to the outcome of elections. You could have a completely neutral districting and end up with a completely partisan outcome. Massachusetts is an example. Massachusetts Republicans are scattered throughout the state, and as a result they are not able to elect one member of the House of Representatives, while at the same time they are quite successful in statewide elections, as evidenced by Governors Weld, Romney, and Baker, all Republicans. The problem is not partisan outcomes but the use of characteristics of the people to place them in legislative districts to secure wins for a particular party or to minimize its losses. It is the use of this information that is the source of the gerrymandering problem. Usually, it is the people's information on party affiliation or voting history, but it could, and probably has, included their income, their occupation, and numerous other aspects of their person. The framers could not have possibly contemplated the use of big data and advanced technology to micromanage the composition of legislative districts. (See O'Neil.)

The question to ask is, how does big data and advanced technology work its magic in districting? The answer is through the placement of small geographical areas with certain personal characteristics in one or another district to enhance the value of those persons' votes or to devalue them with respect to the outcome of an election. The result is geographically contorted districts. Any citizen can look at these district maps and know instantly what is going on. To say that the Supreme Court cannot figure this out is beyond rational comprehension, especially since federal and state courts showed that they were beginning to figure this out. Partisanship is the indicator, but it is not the basis for shaping the remedy. The remedy is to control the geographical contortions of districts by imposing a compactness requirement, much as the Supreme Court imposed the one-person, one-vote rule. Both come from earlier requirements imposed by Congress.

6. The Supreme Court finds it difficult to define what is fair. The *Rucho* majority argued that "it is not even clear what fairness looks like in this context" (*Rucho* majority slip opinion, 17). They do not see how to determine when "a districting map treats a political party fairly" (*Rucho* majority slip opinion, 20). But consider John Rawls's discussion of fairness (he was an American political philosopher famous for his theory of justice). Central to his conception of fairness is the concept that when members of the society are deciding an issue, they are to operate behind a veil of ignorance—that is, they are not to know what their situation will be after the decision. For example, in making districting decisions, the participants are not to know anything about the people except where they live—not their party affiliation, not their voting history, not their income, not their occupation, not anything. Then the decision will be viewed as fair by Rawls's theory of justice. Of course, this is a hypothetical situation. But it suggests that focusing on compactness is a way to provide a remedy that is fair to all parties because it excludes all these personal characteristics from consideration. In addition, it is not necessary to define what is fair, but only to say what is manifestly unfair, a task that the majority even admits to in decrying "results that reasonably seem unjust." Certainly, a districting plan that has a chance of one in a thousand or less of occurring under traditional districting procedures is manifestly unfair. Maybe even one occurring no more often than one in a hundred is manifestly unfair.

The *Rucho* majority is like a repeat of *Colegrove v. Green* in the one-person, one-vote context except now in the gerrymandering context. And Justice Black's dissent in *Colegrove* seems equally applicable here. He stated,

> It is true voting is a part of elections and that elections are "political." But as this court said in *Nixon v. Herndon*, it is a mere "play on words" to refer to a controversy such as this as "political" in the sense that courts have nothing to do in protecting and vindicating the right of a voter to cast an effective ballot." (*Colegrove*, 573)

Perhaps the fate of *Colegrove* will also be the fate of *Rucho v. Common Cause*. Rest assured, the issue of gerrymandering will not go away, as much as the majority in *Rucho* would like to believe that they have put an end to it in federal courts. The similar question involving population disparities did not disappear in the context of *Colegrove*.

What happened after the decision in *Rucho v. Common Cause* in North Carolina is very interesting. Within three months of the Supreme Court's decision in *Rucho v. Common Cause*, a North Carolina three-judge panel state trial court ruled in a pending case over the gerrymandering of the state legislature's two houses that the state's adopted plan was an unconstitutional gerrymander under provisions of the North Carolina Constitution (*Common Cause v. Lewis*). No federal laws or constitutional provisions were involved. The North Carolina court ruled that the gerrymandering violated four different provisions of the North Carolina Constitution. And each violation stood independently from any of the other violations. North Carolina has a constitutional provision stating that "all elections shall be free" (North Carolina Const. Art. I, § 10). The North Carolina court found that the Free Elections Clause of the North Carolina Constitution means that "elections must be conducted freely and honestly to ascertain, fairly and truthfully, the will of the people" (*Common Cause v. Lewis*, Judgment, 300). The court then found as follows:

> [E]xtreme partisan gerrymandering—namely redistricting plans that entrench politicians in power, that evince a fundamental distrust of voters by serving the self interest of political parties over the public good, and that dilute and devalue votes of some citizens compared to others—is contrary to the fundamental right of North

Carolina citizens to have elections conducted freely and honestly to ascertain, fairly and truthfully, the will of the people. Extreme partisan gerrymandering does not fairly and truthfully ascertain the will of the people. Voters are not freely choosing their representatives. Rather, representatives are choosing their voters. It is not the will of the people that is fairly ascertained through extreme partisan gerrymandering. Rather, it is the will of the map drawers that prevails." (*Common Cause v. Lewis*, Judgment, 302)

The North Carolina Constitution guarantees that "no person shall be denied the equal protection of the laws" (North Carolina Const. Art I, § 19). The North Carolina court applied the familiar federal test of a violation of equal protection—namely, that there was a discriminatory intent and a discriminatory effect without a legitimate state interest or other neutral factor justifying such discrimination (*Common Cause v. Lewis*, Judgment, 315). The North Carolina court concluded that the state's Equal Protection Clause was violated "because, by seeking to diminish the electoral power of supporters of a disfavored party, a partisan gerrymander treats individuals who support candidates of one political party less favorably than individuals who support candidates of another party" (*Common Cause v. Lewis*, Judgment, 307).

In addition, the state Constitution's guarantees of free speech and free assembly were found to have been violated by the gerrymander under review.

What was the evidence? It was similar to the evidence presented in *Rucho v. Common Cause*. In fact, many of the same experts testified in *Common Cause v. Lewis*. A telling piece of evidence was presented by Dr. Jowei Chen. The North Carolina court stated that it "gives great weight to Dr. Chen's findings and, to the extent set forth below, adopts his conclusions" (*Common Cause v. Lewis*, Judgment, 40). Dr. Chen drew 1,000 simulated sets of redistricting plans for the North Carolina House and 1,000 sets of simulated districting plans for the North Carolina Senate. In all simulations, Dr. Chen employed traditional districting principles: equal district population, contiguity, compactness, avoiding splitting municipalities, avoiding splitting VTDs (census voting districts), keeping the same county groupings and number of county traversals under the challenged state plan, and maintaining the boundaries of five House districts and four Senate districts ordered by a federal court

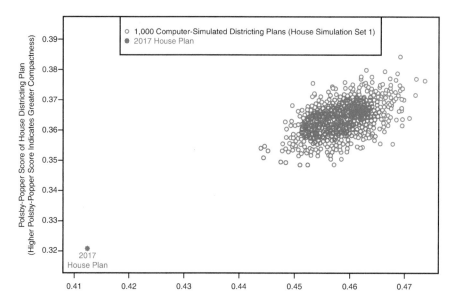

Figure 11 House Simulation Set 1 (Following Only Nonpartisan Redistricting Criteria): Comparison of 2017 House Plan Versus 1,000 Simulated Plans on Compactness.

Reock Score of House districting plan. Higher Reock score indicates greater compactness.
Source: *Common Cause v. Lewis*, Judgment, Plaintiff's Exhibit 14, prepared by Dr. Jowei Chen and reproduced on page 44 of the Judgment.

to remedy a finding of racial discrimination. Figure 11 shows the Reock Compactness Scores and the Polsby-Popper Compactness Scores for the 1,000 House simulation plans and for the state plan being challenged. (Actually, the scores are the average of the individual district scores in each plan.) It is clear to any observer that the state plan fails. Dr. Chen concluded "with over 99% statistical certainty that the enacted House plan subordinates the traditional districting criterion of compactness, and that the current districts are less compact than they would be under a map drawing process that prioritizes and follows the traditional districting criteria" (*Common Cause v. Lewis*, Judgment, 43). There was a virtually identical scattergram for the Senate districts. It is understandable why the court at one point described the evidence of constitutional violation as being "without any reasonable doubt" (*Common Cause v. Lewis*, Judgment, 316).

The North Carolina court enjoined the use of the state's redistricting plans in identified districts, required the entire redistricting process to be conducted in public, and declared the criteria to be used in formulating new plans. In doing so, the court ordered that "[p]artisan considerations and election results data shall not be used in the drawing of legislative districts in the Remedial Maps" (*Common Cause v. Lewis*, Judgment, 355). The other criteria were the same traditional ones employed by Dr. Chen. The court ordered that twenty-one Senate districts in seven county groupings and fifty-six House districts in fourteen other county groupings be redrawn. The defendants did not appeal the court's decision and submitted remedial maps to the court. After reviewing objections made by the plaintiffs and concluding that, notwithstanding those objections, the House and Senate remedial plans "comported" with the court's order on drawing remedial plans, the court approved those plans on October 28, 2019, with an exception for compliance with racial gerrymandering to be addressed in a separate order (not yet issued) (*Common Cause v. Lewis*, Remedial Order). The plaintiffs' objections focused on five county groupings of House districts: Columbus-Pender-Robeson, Forsyth-Yadkin, Cleveland-Gaston, Brunswick–New Hanover, and Guilford. The House districts in these counties are analyzed below.

On September 27, 2019, just twenty-four days after the decision in *Common Cause v. Lewis* concerning state legislative districts in North Carolina, a lawsuit was filed in the North Carolina Superior Court challenging the state's congressional districts, and the case was assigned to the same three-judge trial panel that had decided *Common Cause v. Lewis* (*Harper v. Lewis*). These are the same congressional districts involved in the case that the Supreme Court refused to hear in *Rucho v. Common Cause*. The challenge was based on the same provisions of the North Carolina Constitution that were at issue in the state legislative districts case. The plaintiffs asked for a preliminary injunction preventing the state from proceeding with any administration of the challenged congressional district plan. The court granted the preliminary injunction on October 28, 2019, the same date of the remedial plan's approval in *Common Cause v. Lewis*, finding that the plaintiffs were likely to succeed on the merits and would suffer irreparable loss. In doing so, the court acknowledged that this meant that the status quo in North Carolina would be that there was no congressional district plan in place because the preceding one had been thrown out in federal court over racial gerrymandering. While the court admitted that it had no authority at this stage to order the defendants to develop a new congressional district plan, it urged the state legislature to do so, pointing out that the legislature had recently done so in *Common Cause v. Lewis.*

The legislature adopted a new congressional redistricting plan on November 15, 2019, on a pure party-line vote in both houses of the legislature and in a nontransparent process. The plaintiffs claimed that this remedial plan carried forward the gerrymandering present in the challenged plan. The defendants claimed that the adoption of this plan mooted the plaintiffs' case. Without deciding these issues and leaving competing motions for summary judgment pending, the court issued an order on December 2, 2019, allowing the state Board of Elections to accept filings for candidacies for congressional districts under the November 2019 plan. It is unclear what this all meant for the 2020 elections and for the reapportionment coming after the 2020 Census. The 2020 elections did go ahead under the November plan, but the court may establish *Common Cause v. Lewis* standards for reapportionment.

6

Manageable Standard for Resolving Gerrymandering

Gerrymandering litigation has been focused on partisanship. But that is not the only type of gerrymandering that can occur. Legislative districts could be assembled so that the votes of persons of above-average income were overvalued and those of persons of below-average income were undervalued. Other factors could be the presence of children or the owners of property. The intent and the effect of a violation of a protected right can be established and remedied by focusing on the mechanism by which all gerrymanders operate. This is the distortion of the geography of legislative districts. Here is where the test of compliance is to be found. It is not whether the outcome reflects some partisanship or the spatial distribution of income has some variation. Those results can occur in a neutral, unbiased set of legislative districts. Compliance needs to be judged on the absence of the mechanism through which unacceptable gerrymandering operates.

How is this to be achieved? As seen above, gerrymanders are implemented by causing legislative districts to take unusual shapes that might lead even the uninitiated to wonder, what has this pattern got to do with anything? Of course, it has to do with altering the electoral outcome by marshaling voters on the basis of the voters' personal characteristics. The key to measuring compliance is to exclude all voter personal characteristics from the districting process.

The steps for testing the compliance of proposed districting plans are as follows:

1. Define what constitutes an acceptable districting process.
2. Create a large number of simulated districting plans using the process defined in step one. This should be large enough for statistical purposes; a simulation set of at least 500 alternative districting plans is recommended.
3. Select a measure of the performance of each of the simulated plans, the challenged plan, and any proposed remedial plans.
4. Define what plans are acceptable.
5. Apply the definition of acceptability to evaluate the challenged plan and any proposed remedial plans.

The first step delineates criteria that can be used to create acceptable districting plans without the use of any characteristics of the persons in any geographic area, including their partisan behavior. These criteria have been frequently mentioned in various judicial opinions. They are:

a. **Equal population.** Each district within a state shall comply with the one-person, one-vote requirement.
b. **Contiguity.** Each part of a district shall be contiguous to another part of the same district. This could include a requirement that the contiguity be meaningful, such as requiring a boundary of some minimal length.
c. **Compactness.** Districts shall be compact. Courts have increasingly come to rely on the Reock Compactness Score and the Polsby-Popper Compactness Score as measures of compactness.
d. **Minimize census voting district (VTD) splits.** Use reasonable efforts to avoid splitting a VTD between districts.
e. **Minimize municipal splits.** Use reasonable efforts to avoid splitting a municipality between districts.
f. **Comply with outstanding court orders.** This generally involves preserving the boundaries established in court orders under the Voting Rights Act of 1965.

Common Cause v. Lewis also permitted the protection of incumbents by allowing districts to be drawn so that incumbents did not have to face each other in an election. Since this process is a framework for testing constitutional compliance and there is no constitutional right for an incumbent to avoid facing another incumbent as a result of redistricting, protection of incumbents is inappropriate. Including protection of incumbents serves to enshrine the results of the current gerrymandered districts and their antecedents. To test a districting plan against a simulation set that protects incumbents provides a device for extreme gerrymandering to hide behind the protection of incumbents. This is not to say that protecting incumbents is offensive, but rather to say that the test of acceptable plans should be against a simulation set that does not protect incumbents, because some of that set will also protect incumbents.

Step Two involves creating a set of alternative districting plans by simulating the districting process using advanced computer technology and an algorithm implementing the process laid out in step one. (See Chen and Rodden; Vickery.) While the skills needed to generate these alternative plans are not possessed by everybody, they are widely available and have been utilized in numerous gerrymandering cases. These alternative sets of legislative districts make up a sample of the full set of districts that would meet the requirements of the process in step one. As such, the number of simulations must be sufficient to generate a reliable sample. A size of 500 simulated districting plans is recommended.

The third step is to settle upon a measure to be used to compare various districting plans. All the criteria set forth in step one are taken into account in all the simulations. To select a measure of performance, it is important to focus on the mechanism that gerrymandering uses to accomplish its unconstitutional districting, namely the creation of geographically contorted districts. The measure that best suits the purpose will largely capture the extent of these distortions. That measure is one of the compactness of the set of districts in a plan. There are many possible measures of compactness, but as discussed earlier, two have become widely used in recent court decisions: the Reock Compactness Score and the Polsby-Popper Compactness Score. For each of these, a higher score indicates more compactness. The Reock Compactness Score focuses on the area within a district in comparison to the area of the smallest encircling circle, and the Polsby-Popper Compactness Score focuses on the area within a district compared to the area of a circle with a circumference equal to the district's perimeter. So, they each measure different aspects of compactness. The Reock Compactness Score is a dispersion measure; it measures how spread out the geography of a district is. The Polsby-Popper Compactness Score is a perimeter measure; it is sensitive to perimeter irregularities, in contrast to the Reock Compactness Score, which is insensitive to perimeter irregularities. To capture these two basic aspects of geographic distortion, two measures are required. If the simulated plans are ranked from highest to lowest scores for each measure, they do not produce identical, or even highly correlated, rankings of the alternative simulated plans. But together they identify the feasible set of compliant districting plans.

In addition to representing the geographic distortions underlying gerrymandering, compactness was identified by Congress in the 1911 Apportionment Act as one of the criteria to be used in defining congressional districts. And the constitutions of twenty-five states contain a requirement that compactness be used in districting of state legislatures.

Reock Compactness Scores and Polsby-Popper Compactness Scores are calculated for each district in a districting plan for a state. (See above for definitions of these scores.) The Reock Compactness Score for all districts in a particular simulated or challenged/remedial plan is calculated by adding together all the Reock Compactness Scores for the districts in a specific plan and dividing the result by the number of districts in that plan. It is the average of the scores of the districts in that plan. The Polsby-Popper Compactness Score for a specific plan is calculated similarly. As a result, there are two scores for each district in a districting plan and two average scores for all the districts in that plan. This is important because sometimes the litigation focuses on a specific district or group of districts. The analysis can be carried out for either of them.

The fourth step is to delineate the set of districting plans that are acceptable. Consider the statewide status of a districting plan for the moment. The average of the Reock Compactness Scores for all the districts in a particular statewide plan and the average of the Polsby-Popper Compactness Scores for all the districts in that particular statewide plan are plotted on a graph (a scattergram). Next, plot the same set of two scores for each simulated plan. The resultant plot outlines the area of acceptable districting plans. Figures 6, 7, and 11 are examples of such graphs. (For the moment, ignore the nonsimulated point—namely, the averages of the Reock Compactness Scores and the Polsby-Popper Compactness Scores for the districts in the districting plan being challenged.)

The cluster of points in the upper right area of these figures represents the districting plans that are generated by districting criteria described in step one. If a plan should produce a set of scores that appear in the general area of the scattergram to the right of the smallest Polsby-Popper Compactness Score and above the smallest Reock Compactness Score for the simulated plans, that plan would have a set of scores for a sufficiently compliant plan. The scattergram and these hypothetical outcomes together define a *zone of acceptance.*

This zone can be more precisely defined by using statistical methods. Consider the distribution of Reock Compactness Scores for all the simulated plans; by grouping these scores in intervals, the results can be illustrated as a histogram. These histograms approximate a normal distribution. The same can be done for the Polsby-Popper Compactness Scores. In addition, for each of the Reock and Polsby-Popper Compactness Scores, there are summary statistics, namely the mean, standard deviation, minimum, and maximum. The normal distribution has two tails, areas where the probability of an observation occurring is small. In the present case, only the tail at the low end of values is of interest because the investigation is into the occurrence of observations that are too small, indicating gerrymandering. The properties of the normal distribution are that the probability that an observation would occur at a value more than 2.3263 standard deviations below the average value for that set of simulations is 1.00 percent, one chance in a hundred. All sets of scores that have a Reock Compactness Score greater than the average Reock Compactness Score for that set of simulations minus 2.3263 times its standard deviation and a Polsby-Popper Compactness Score that is greater than the average Polsby-Popper Compactness Score for that set of simulations minus 2.3263 times its standard deviation precisely define the zone of acceptance. Note that there is a nonzero probability that the simulations may generate one or more points outside the zone of acceptance, but the likelihood is small.

If a challenged plan's set of scores is in this zone of acceptance, the challenge should fail, as it is not gerrymandered as alleged, regardless of whether the plan produces a partisan result. Likewise, if a remedial plan's set of scores is in this zone of acceptance, it has acceptably corrected the violations in the challenged plan.

Next, sets of scores that are outside the zone of acceptance need to be interpreted. The remaining unassigned area is divided by locating the values at which parts of those areas have a probability of observation below 0.2 percent, or one in 500, a rare enough event to make a districting plan unacceptable. That occurs when a Reock Compactness Score is less than the Reock Compactness Score's average minus 2.8782 times its standard deviation, *or* a Polsby-Popper Compactness Score is less than the Polsby-Popper Compactness Score's average minus 2.8782 times its standard deviation. In addition, any set of scores appearing with a Reock Compactness Score of less than the Reock Compactness Score's average minus 2.3263 times its standard deviation *and* a Polsby-Popper Compactness Score of less than the Polsby-Popper Compactness Score's average minus 2.3263 times its standard deviation has a probability of occurring that is less than 0.01 percent, or one chance in 10,000. Scores with low values in these areas constitute the *zone of unacceptance.*

The remaining unassigned area constitutes an *intermediate zone* that is considered more thoroughly in the following discussion. These zones are illustrated in Figure 12.

Some may object to the probability basis of these boundaries. But the presence of probability cannot be avoided. Even in the context of one-person, one-vote, probability plays a role, although more easily camouflaged or ignored. The census population numbers are not an actual 100 percent accurate count. There is error in the conduct of the census. This should not be a surprise for an effort as large and complicated as the census. For example, the 1990 Census had an error of 1.61 percent, and the 2000 Census had one of 0.49 percent (Mulry). The most common standard for statistical significance is 95 percent, which would find a set of scores a constitutional violation if that set were only 5 percent or less likely to occur. In the present situation, the test is even more stringent in that a set of scores would have to occur with a less than 0.2 percent likelihood to be found a constitutional violation.

The result divides the scattergram into three zones for analysis: (a) the zone of acceptance, (b) an intermediate zone, and (c) the zone of unacceptance. Districting plans with sets of compactness scores in the zone of acceptance should be approved. Districting plans with sets of compactness scores in the zone of unacceptance should be rejected. Districting plans that have sets of compactness scores in the intermediate zone should be treated on the basis of how the plans got there. If the plan

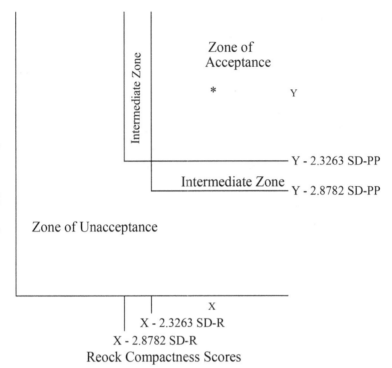

Polsby-Popper Compactness Scores

Intermediate Zone

Zone of
Acceptance

*   Y

————— Y - 2.3263 SD-PP
Intermediate Zone — Y - 2.8782 SD-PP

Zone of Unacceptance

X
X - 2.3263 SD-R
X - 2.8782 SD-R
Reock Compactness Scores

* is the intersection point of the average of the Reock Compactness Scores (X)
and the average of the Polsby-Popper Compactness Scores (Y) for 1,000
simulations using traditional districting criteria (Step One Criteria).
That is, no incumbent protection or similar criteria.

SD-PP is the standard deviation of the Polsby-Popper Compactness
Scores in the simulation.

SD-R is the standard deviation of the Reock Compactness
Scores in the simulation.

Figure 12 Manageable Standard for Evaluating Gerrymandering
Using Traditional Districting Criteria to Simulate the Zone of Acceptable
Districting Plans (That Is, No Incumbent or Similar Protections).

was the one being challenged, it depends on the reasons for its being
located there and whether those reasons stand up to scrutiny. Such a
challenged plan could be given the benefit of the doubt and be reluc-
tantly approved if, for example, it was the result of a truly nonpartisan
selection process receiving support from all interested groups. But if it is
a remedial plan following a determination of a constitutional violation,
it should not receive the benefit of the doubt and should be scrutinized

more closely. Part of determining whether to accept a remedial plan located in the intermediate zone would be whether the plan has received meaningful bipartisan support from the legislature, not just from a committee and not just token bipartisan support. If it has, that remedial plan could be approved. If it has not, it should be rejected.

A court could utilize a stricter version of this methodology by eliminating the intermediate zone and adding its area to the zone of unacceptable plans. Then, all plans that were less likely than one in a hundred to occur would be rejected as unacceptable. Furthermore, a court could apply the more stringent standard to congressional districts and the three-zone standard to state legislative districts. Such an approach mirrors the treatment in the one-person, one-vote cases.

Similar scattergrams and analysis can be done for individual districts or groups of districts. However, when doing so, it is important to be aware that a district cannot be changed without affecting at least one other district. As a result, it is not possible to analyze one district in isolation from the others. The change made to improve the one district may have unduly harmed another one. At a minimum, all the districts being affected by alternative districts must be analyzed together and individually. In addition, another decision rule should come into play—namely, that the changes do not make the overall compliance worse for the group of districts or state as a whole.

Now that the evaluation process has been established, the problem created by protecting incumbents from facing each other can be demonstrated. A comparison of Figures 6 and 7 illustrates the problem created by protecting incumbents in a simulation. Figure 6 is a simulation set that does not include protection of incumbents. Figure 7 is a simulation set in the same state that does protect incumbents. The simulation set that protects incumbents moves the scattergram of simulated plans to the left and downward, making it easier for an offending districting plan to get through scrutiny. The Polsby-Popper lowest simulated score drops from about 0.29 to 0.19, and the lowest Reock simulated score drops from about 0.355 to 0.33. As a result, all of the simulated plans protecting incumbents have a set of scores outside the area of acceptance indicated in the simulated set that does not protect incumbents. A simulation to examine the protection of incumbents should be constrained to only permit sets of scores that are in the area of acceptance identified in the simulation set that did not protect incumbents. If plans to protect incumbents cannot be at least that acceptable, the plans to protect incumbents are too corrupted by past gerrymandering to be protected any further. That closes or restricts the back door of incumbency protection to unacceptable districting plans.

How does this approach fare for the cases for which there is sufficient information to apply it? Unfortunately, the information on the standard deviations of the scores in the sets of simulated plans is not available. As a result, the precise boundaries of the three zones cannot be drawn on these simulations. However, it is possible to infer some conclusions.

The scattergrams in Figures 6 and 7 for the Pennsylvania case show clearly that the challenged plan is an extreme gerrymander, with it appearing in the unacceptance zone of Figure 6, the simulation without incumbent protection, and so extremely gerrymandered that it could not even pass muster in Figure 7, the simulation protecting incumbents. The plan challenged in Pennsylvania was so extremely gerrymandered that the bias of past gerrymanders permitted in Figure 7 could not save it. How does the remedial plan adopted by the Pennsylvania Supreme Court measure up under this analysis? The Reock Compactness Score for the remedial plan is 0.46, and its Polsby-Popper Compactness Score is 0.33 (*League of Women Voters of Pennsylvania v. Commonwealth of Pennsylvania*, Measures of Compactness). As was mentioned above, this point is located well within the acceptance zone in Figure 6 as well as Figure 7 and is a clear improvement over the challenged plan.

It is also the case that a brighter line might be called for in congressional districting, much as has evolved over time in the one-person, one-vote area. Such a line would require acceptable plans to actually have sets of compactness scores in the zone of acceptance.

What is the result of applying this process to the state legislative district challenge in North Carolina? In North Carolina, the court ordered that the districts in specified county groupings (in actuality, some were single counties with multiple districts) be redrawn. Since adjustments were confined to each county grouping, each county group could be adjusted independently from all the others. To carry out the process of redistricting, the House and Senate each selected a base map for every county grouping, which map was then modified. The state house used county group specific base maps from Dr. Chen's simulations with no incumbency protection (*Common Cause v. Lewis*, Remedial Order, 5). Although there is limited information (i.e., lack of mean and standard

deviation for the simulated set of plans) for applying the standard developed here, some inferences are possible with the information that is
available.

Since the House started with a base map selected from the simulation set with no incumbency protection, it is nearly certain that at
the outset the plan for each county group was located in the zone of
acceptance. The plaintiffs challenged the remedial plan for five county
groups containing nineteen House districts. The plaintiffs submitted additional information on these five county groups, including an
additional report by Dr. Chen. From this information, we have some
details on the Reock and Polsby-Popper Compactness Scores for the
districts in each of these county groups, including the scattergram for
each. Unfortunately, the scattergrams are for a simulation set that protects incumbents. Three of the county groups had scores that placed
them in the zone of acceptance of the incumbent-protected simulations (Columbus-Pender-Robeson, Cleveland-Gaston, and Brunswick–
New Hanover), but it is difficult to say where they were located on a
scattergram for a simulation set that did not protect incumbents. The
Reock and Polsby-Popper Compactness Scores for the Brunswick–New
Hanover group appear likely to be in such a simulation set's zone of
acceptance. The incumbency-protected simulation scattergrams for the
other two groups show that the remedial plans for them are likely in
that unprotected-incumbent set's zone of unacceptance. Many of the
plaintiffs' objections to the five county groups are in terms of the partisanship of the remedial plan's districts in these county groups. But it
is important to remember that resolving gerrymanders does not mean
that partisan outcomes are eliminated. It is interesting to note that all
of these remedial county group plans were adopted unanimously by the
House districting committee (ten Republicans and seven Democrats),
except for the plan for Columbus-Pender-Robeson, which was adopted
on a party-line vote. The court rejected all of these challenges to the
House's remedial plan. The flaw in this case was analyzing compliance
using a biased incumbent-protecting simulation set, especially since the
House elected to use as its base plans ones that were not incumbency
protected.

The State Senate used county group specific base maps selected
from Dr. Chen's simulation with incumbency protection. The plaintiffs
raised no objections to the remedial plan for the State Senate. However,

based on the discussion of the biases introduced by utilizing a simulation set that protects incumbents, it is likely that the Senate remedial plan would be found deficient in the absence of incumbency protection.

The courts should require that a certain minimum amount of information be provided in implementing the standard proposed here. In particular, the following should be provided for each set of simulations (including for ones scrutinizing a specific district or group of districts): the scattergram and the histogram, mean, median, minimum, maximum, and standard deviation of the Reock Compactness Scores and of the Polsby-Popper Compactness Scores for that simulation.

This process provides evidence of whether there is a violation of constitutional law and is a means of assessing the adequacy of remedial plans.

Conclusion

The logjam blocking action to remedy inequities in the allocation of voting rights across state legislative and congressional districts within a state was removed by the Supreme Court's decision in *Baker v. Carr*. The impediment was something called the nonjusticiability of political questions. *Baker v. Carr* held that allegations that the value of votes is diluted by having some districts within the state with more people in them than other districts did not constitute a nonjusticiable political question. In doing so, the Supreme Court set forth a test for nonjusticiable political questions as including one or more of the following six factors:

1. "[A] textually demonstrable constitutional commitment of the issue to a coordinate political department"
2. "[A] lack of judicially discoverable and manageable standards for resolving it"
3. "[T]he impossibility of deciding without an initial policy determination of a kind clearly for nonjudicial discretion"
4. "[T]he impossibility of a court's undertaking independent resolution without expressing lack of the respect due coordinate branches of government"
5. "[A]n unusual need for unquestioning adherence to a political decision already made"
6. "[T]he potentiality of embarrassment from multifarious pronouncements by various departments on one question" (*Baker v. Carr*, 217)

Five of these factors are true to the Supreme Court's statement that "it is the relationship between the judiciary and the coordinate branches of the Federal Government . . . which gives rise to the political question" (*Baker v. Carr*, 210). But the second factor, namely the "lack of judicially discoverable and manageable standards for resolving it," is not. It does not belong on this list of factors determining what is a political question. It does not involve any other branch of the federal government. It only involves the judiciary and, as such, is no more than an excuse for the judiciary to avoid doing its job: to decide hard cases as well as easy ones. Without this factor, all the voting rights cases are clearly justiciable, as they clearly should be.

Following *Baker v. Carr*, the Supreme Court established a standard for reviewing allegations that congressional districts in a state and a state's legislative districts were malapportioned—that is, that districts did not have equal populations. The standard is the well-known one-person, one-vote rule. In applying this standard, a near-mathematical equality was required in congressional district cases based on a violation of Article I, Section 2, with more leeway allowed in state legislative districts based on a violation of the Equal Protection Clause (generally accepting a 10 percent population discrepancy). More interesting is the history of this phrase used by the Supreme Court: "as nearly as is practicable one man's vote in a congressional election is to be worth as much as another's" (*Wesberry v. Sanders*). The phrase "as nearly as is practicable" is nearly verbatim from the Apportionment Act of 1911, which required congressional districts to be a "contiguous and compact territory, and containing as nearly as practicable an equal number of inhabitants."

Following the one-person, one-vote litigation, plaintiffs attacked the process of distorting district boundaries, known as gerrymandering. These attacks have relied principally on the Equal Protection Clause but also raised claims under the Elections Clause (Article I) and the First Amendment. In general, if there is discriminatory intent and effect, the Equal Protection Clause is violated unless there is a rational relationship to a legitimate governmental interest. What is the legitimate governmental interest in constructing legislative districts so as to favor one group over another? There is no legitimate governmental interest in this activity. In fact, there is no governmental interest at all. It is only in the interest of a group, usually a political party, and not any governmental entity. It is a use of the governmental process to achieve a purely private end. It is not that acceptable districts cannot be partisan, but that partisanship cannot subordinate the legitimate governmental interests in districting decisions.

What are the legitimate governmental interests in districting decisions? What are the fundamental aspects of districting decisions? The Pennsylvania Supreme Court identified these interests as district contiguity, compactness, and population equality. Its decision not only identified these fundamental interests but also demonstrated that a judiciously discoverable and manageable standard exists. Congress recognized these three fundamental standards in the Apportionment Act of 1911. There is no reason why the Supreme Court could not turn to Congress's 1911 action as guidance to what the fundamental interests are. After all, it essentially did this in crafting the one-person, one-vote rule. If these three fundamental interests are subordinated to partisanship or any other interest, there is a violation of the Equal Protection Clause because partisanship or these other interests are not rationally related to the districting process. Furthermore, partisanship is not a legitimate governmental interest justifying such a violation.

Adherence to political subdivisions can be a possible justification for unusual deviations from sensible districting. It could be part of the standard for determining whether there is a constitutional violation.

In *Rucho v. Common Cause*, the Supreme Court stepped away from its earlier decisions finding gerrymandering cases to be justiciable. In *Rucho*, it held them to be nonjusticiable political questions because there is no judicially discernable and manageable standard. As has been shown in the preceding pages, the Supreme Court's reasons for this 5–4 decision do not stand up to scrutiny. One consequence has been increased activity in state courts under state constitutional provisions. North Carolina is a prime example of this, as is the Pennsylvania case that preceded the Supreme Court's decision. Twenty-five states have constitutional provisions like either Pennsylvania's or North Carolina's. Some of these states also require compactness, along with an additional fourteen that require compactness. That makes thirty-nine states that have either Pennsylvania's constitutional provision, North Carolina's constitutional provision, or a constitutional provision requiring compactness.

Even if the requirement for a judicially discernible and manageable standard is accepted as a part of the test for a nonjusticiable political question, the existence of such a test has been demonstrated in these pages. This standard for resolving gerrymandering claims focuses on the mechanism that is utilized to implement gerrymandering—namely, the distortion of the boundaries of districts—and looks to past congressional acts for guidance. The key to a manageable standard is compactness and advanced technology. There are five steps:

1. Identify acceptable districting plans based on six measures: equal populations, contiguity, compactness, minimizing census voting district splits, minimizing municipal boundary splits, and complying with outstanding court orders under the Voting Rights Act.

2. Create a large number (at least 500) of simulated alternative district plans that comply with these measures and do not protect incumbents.

3. Use two measures of compactness (the Reock Compactness Score and the Polsby-Popper Compactness Score) to compare alternative simulated districts, challenged districts, and remedial plan districts.

4. Create a scattergram of the two compactness scores for the set of simulated plans. The scattergram is divided into three different zones (see Figure 12). Sets of compactness scores located in the zone of acceptance are not gerrymandered, those located in the zone of unacceptance are gerrymandered, and those located in the intermediate zone are categorized depending on how they got there.

5. Locate the challenged or remedial plans on the scattergram, and treat them on the basis of which zone they are located in. This process eliminates excessive partisan gerrymandering. It is politically neutral, as called for by Justice Kennedy in *Vieth* and the majority in *Rucho v. Common Cause* (quoting Justice Kennedy) (*Rucho v. Common Cause*, majority slip opinion, 15).

This standard is easily implemented. It would straighten out the gerrymandering controversies as rapidly as the equal population standard did for the earlier population disparity problem.

APPENDIX A

Congressional Districting Following the 1800 Census: Population Disparities and Geographical Distortions

Upon completion of the 1800 Census, Congress adopted in 1802 an act to apportion the representatives of the House of Representatives among the several states (Act for the Apportionment . . .). As a part of this legislation, the size of the House was increased by thirty-five members. According to this act, the members of the House of Representatives were apportioned among the several states as follows:

Connecticut	7
Delaware	1
Georgia	4
Kentucky	6
Maryland	9
Massachusetts	17
New Hampshire	5
New Jersey	6
New York	17
North Carolina	12
Pennsylvania	18

Rhode Island	2
South Carolina	8
Tennessee	3
Vermont	4
Virginia	22

(There has been debate over when Ohio was admitted with one member in the House, which debate was not settled until legislation passed in 1953.) The House was increased to 141 members (142 if Ohio is counted).

How did the states go about electing members of the House of Representatives? Six states elected their members in statewide at-large elections (Connecticut, Georgia, New Hampshire, New Jersey, Rhode Island, and Tennessee), and Delaware and Ohio each had only one representative. The remainder divided their states into nonoverlapping geographical districts and elected representatives from these districts. Some districts in a few states elected more than one member to the House (multimember districts). Each of these states is examined to see how they fared against the modern-day standard on one person, one vote.

The states using districts to elect members of the House of Representatives generally followed county boundaries, but in some cases, counties were divided among two or more districts. With one exception in a New York district, all parts of a district were contiguous with at least one other part of the district. Maps of the congressional districts in the states analyzed are presented at the end of this Appendix. As discussed in the text, the modern standard for congressional districts is near-mathematical equality in number of persons across districts within the same state. State legislative districting is given more leeway, with up to a 10 percent discrepancy needing no justification.

The 1800 Census enumerated the number of persons, including the number of slaves. However, the Constitution required that for apportionment of the House of Representatives, slaves were to be counted as three-fifths of a person. As a result, the population figures from the Census had to be adjusted so that only three-fifths of the slaves were counted for apportionment purposes.

The examination of states electing representatives from districts proceeds by state in alphabetical order.

KENTUCKY

The adjusted populations of Kentucky's six congressional districts are shown in Table A-1.

Table A-1   Adjusted Populations of Kentucky's Congressional Districts in the Eighth Congress (1803–1805)

District Number	Adjusted Population
1	29,584
2	33,197
3	38,508
4	35,033
5	36,760
6	31,630

Sources: "Mapping Early American Elections," Eighth Congress (1803–1805); U.S. Bureau of the Census, *Population of States and Counties of the United States: 1790–1990* (March 1996); and U.S. Bureau of the Census, *Return of the Whole Number of Persons within the Several Districts of the United States*, 1800 Census of Population.

The minimum and maximum adjusted populations of a Kentucky congressional district were 29,584 and 38,508, respectively. Using the metrics typically relied upon by the Supreme Court in one-person, one-vote cases, the difference between the smallest- and largest-populated districts as a percentage of the ideal mathematical population equivalent (the state's adjusted population divided by the number of members) was 26 percent, and the ratio of the largest-populated district to the smallest-populated district was 1.31. Neither of these comes close to complying with today's requirements for congressional districts. (If these calculations were based on the number of whole persons, the results are similar, with the percentage of the ideal being 29 percent and the ratio being 1.35.)

MARYLAND

The adjusted populations of Maryland's eight congressional districts for electing nine members of the House of Representatives are shown in Table A-2. Maryland districting involved two distinct features. One district (Number 5) elected two members of the House of Representatives. Therefore, it is represented by the adjusted population per member in comparison across districts. The other involved splitting one

Table A-2 Populations of Maryland's Congressional Districts in the Eighth Congress (1803–1805)

District Number	Adjusted Population	Number of Members	Adjusted Population per Member
1	33,145	1	33,145
2	35,028	1	35,028
3	33,055	1	33,055
4	33,055	1	33,055
5	55,161	2	27,581
6	34,078	1	34,078
7	32,256	1	32,256
8	43,516	1	43,516

Sources: "Mapping Early American Elections," Eighth Congress (1803–1805); U.S. Bureau of the Census, *Population of States and Counties of the United States: 1790–1990* (March 1996); and U.S. Bureau of the Census, *Return of the Whole Number of Persons within the Several Districts of the United States*, 1800 Census of Population.

county between two districts (Numbers 3 and 4), with no census detail below the county level. These two districts were combined, and each was assigned one half of the combined adjusted population.

The minimum and maximum adjusted populations of Maryland congressional districts were 27,581 and 43,516, respectively. The difference between the smallest- and largest-populated districts as a percentage of the ideal mathematical population equivalent (the state's adjusted population divided by the number of members) was 48 percent, and the ratio of the largest-populated district to the smallest-populated district was 1.58. Neither of these comes close to complying with today's requirements for congressional districts. (If these calculations were based on the number of whole persons, the results are similar, with the percentage of the ideal being 54 percent and the ratio being 1.7.)

MASSACHUSETTS

The populations of Massachusetts's seventeen congressional districts are shown in Table A-3. In 1800, Massachusetts had no slaves, and therefore the whole number of persons and the adjusted population were identical. At that time, Massachusetts included what is Maine today. The minimum and maximum populations of a Massachusetts congressional district were

Table A-3 Populations of Massachusetts's Congressional Districts in the Eighth Congress (1803–1805)

District Number	Population
1	32,939
2	31,370
3	31,851
4	34,863
5	37,471
6	34,961
7	30,073
8	32,389
9	29,519
10	28,135
11	33,057
12	33,885
13	32,332
14	37,896
15	38,208
16	30,225
17	45,390

Sources: "Mapping Early American Elections," Eighth Congress (1803–1805); U.S. Bureau of the Census, *Population of States and Counties of the United States: 1790–1990* (March 1996); and U.S. Bureau of the Census, *Return of the Whole Number of Persons within the Several Districts of the United States*, 1800 Census of Population.

28,135 and 45,390, respectively. The difference between the smallest- and largest-populated districts as a percentage of the ideal mathematical population equivalent (the state's population divided by the number of members) was 51 percent, and the ratio of the largest-populated district to the smallest-populated district was 1.61. Neither of these comes close to complying with today's requirements for congressional districts.

NEW YORK

The adjusted populations of New York's seventeen congressional districts are shown in Table A-4. Two counties were split between two districts (Numbers 2 and 3 and Numbers 11 and 15) without sufficient

Table A-4 Adjusted Populations of New York's Congressional Districts in the Eighth Congress (1803–1805)

District Number	Adjusted Population
1	35,686
2	34,404
3	34,404
4	33,002
5	28,897
6	47,131
7	36,818
8	34,884
9	33,380
10	29,995
11	34,815
12	35,760
13	31,531
14	31,546
15	34,815
16	30,877
17	32,860

Sources: "Mapping Early American Elections," Eighth Congress (1803–1805); U.S. Bureau of the Census, *Population of States and Counties of the United States: 1790–1990* (March 1996); and U.S. Bureau of the Census, *Return of the Whole Number of Persons within the Several Districts of the United States*, 1800 Census of Population.

census detail to divide the counties between districts. These pairs of districts were combined, and each was assigned one half of the pair's combined adjusted population. The minimum and maximum adjusted populations of a New York congressional district were 28,897 and 47,131, respectively. The difference between the smallest- and largest-populated districts as a percentage of the ideal mathematical population equivalent (the state's adjusted population divided by the number of members) was 53 percent, and the ratio of the largest-populated district to the smallest-populated district was 1.63. Neither of these comes close to complying with today's requirements for congressional districts.

(If these calculations were based on the number of whole persons, the results are virtually identical, with the percentage of the ideal being 53 percent and the ratio being 1.63.)

NORTH CAROLINA

The adjusted populations of North Carolina's twelve congressional districts are shown in Table A-5.

The minimum and maximum adjusted populations of a North Carolina congressional district were 31,649 and 39,170, respectively. The difference between the smallest- and largest-populated districts as a percentage of the ideal mathematical population equivalent (the state's adjusted population divided by the number of members) was 21 percent, and the ratio of the largest-populated district to the smallest-populated district was 1.24. Neither of these comes close to complying with today's

Table A-5 Adjusted Populations of North Carolina's Congressional Districts in the Eighth Congress (1803–1805)

District Number	Adjusted Population
1	34,120
2	34,877
3	31,649
4	34,760
5	31,990
6	33,439
7	39,170
8	37,414
9	38,850
10	33,382
11	37,647
12	37,486

Sources: "Mapping Early American Elections," Eighth Congress (1803–1805); U.S. Bureau of the Census, *Population of States and Counties of the United States: 1790–1990* (March 1996); and U.S. Bureau of the Census, *Return of the Whole Number of Persons within the Several Districts of the United States*, 1800 Census of Population.

requirements for congressional districts. (If these calculations were based on the number of whole persons, the results are similar, with the percentage of the ideal being 19 percent and the ratio being 1.21.)

PENNSYLVANIA

The adjusted populations of Pennsylvania's eleven congressional districts for electing eighteen members of the House of Representatives are shown in Table A-6. Four districts elected more than one member to the House of Representatives; Districts 1, 2, and 3 each elected three members to the House, and District 4 elected two members. Therefore, these districts are represented by the adjusted population per member in comparison across districts. In addition, parts of six counties are in more than one district, with no census detail below the county level, necessitating the combination of Districts 2, 4, 5, and 8, and assigning the per member adjusted population to each of these districts.

The minimum and maximum adjusted populations of a Pennsylvania congressional district were 28,264 and 38,738, respectively. The difference

Table A-6 Adjusted Populations of Pennsylvania's Congressional Districts in the Eighth Congress (1803–1805)

District Number	Adjusted Population	Number of Members	Adjusted Population per Member
1	93,781	3	31,260
2	102,700	3	34.233
3	107,806	3	35,935
4	68,467	2	34,234
5	34,234	1	34,234
6	38,738	1	38,738
7	31,603	1	31,603
8	34,234	1	34,234
9	28,718	1	28,718
10	28,264	1	28,264
11	33,145	1	33,145

Sources: "Mapping Early American Elections," Eighth Congress (1803–1805); U.S. Bureau of the Census, *Population of States and Counties of the United States: 1790–1990* (March 1996); and U.S. Bureau of the Census, *Return of the Whole Number of Persons within the Several Districts of the United States*, 1800 Census of Population.

between the smallest- and largest-populated districts as a percentage of the ideal mathematical population equivalent (the state's adjusted population divided by the number of members) was 31 percent, and the ratio of the largest-populated district to the smallest-populated district was 1.37. Neither of these comes close to complying with today's requirements for congressional districts. (If these calculations were based on the number of whole persons, the results are virtually identical, with the percentage of the ideal being 31 percent and the ratio being 1.37.)

SOUTH CAROLINA

The adjusted populations of South Carolina's twelve congressional districts are shown in Table A-7.

The minimum and maximum adjusted populations of a South Carolina congressional district were 30,090 and 40,702, respectively. The difference between the smallest- and largest-populated districts as a percentage of the ideal mathematical population equivalent (the state's adjusted population divided by the number of members) was 30 percent, and the ratio of the largest-populated district to the smallest-populated district was 1.35. Neither of these comes close to complying with today's requirements for congressional districts. (If these calculations were based on the number of whole persons, the results are considerably worse, with the percentage of the ideal being 60 percent and the ratio being 1.82.)

Table A-7 Adjusted Populations of South Carolina's Congressional Districts in the Eighth Congress (1803–1805)

District Number	Adjusted Population
1	40,702
2	36,844
3	33,955
4	35,223
5	36,445
6	35,532
7	38,340
8	30,090

Sources: "Mapping Early American Elections," Eighth Congress (1803–1805); U.S. Bureau of the Census, *Population of States and Counties of the United States: 1790–1990* (March 1996); and U.S. Bureau of the Census, *Return of the Whole Number of Persons within the Several Districts of the United States*, 1800 Census of Population.

VERMONT

The adjusted populations of Vermont's four congressional districts are shown in Table A-8. In 1800, Vermont had no slaves, and therefore the whole number of persons and the adjusted population were identical.

The minimum and maximum populations of a Vermont congressional district were 30,533 and 50,525, respectively. The difference between the smallest- and largest-populated districts as a percentage of the ideal mathematical population equivalent (the state's population divided by the number of members) was 52 percent, and the ratio of the largest-populated district to the smallest-populated district was 1.65. Neither of these comes close to complying with today's requirements for congressional districts.

Table A-8 Adjusted Populations of Vermont's Congressional Districts in the Eighth Congress (1803–1805)

District Number	Adjusted Population
1	38,430
2	50,525
3	30,533
4	34,977

Sources: "Mapping Early American Elections," Eighth Congress (1803–1805); U.S. Bureau of the Census, *Population of States and Counties of the United States: 1790–1990* (March 1996); and U.S. Bureau of the Census, *Return of the Whole Number of Persons within the Several Districts of the United States*, 1800 Census of Population.

VIRGINIA

The adjusted populations of Virginia's twenty-two congressional districts are shown in Table A-9.

The minimum and maximum adjusted populations of a Virginia congressional district were 25,438 and 42,327, respectively. The difference between the smallest- and largest-populated districts as a percentage of the ideal mathematical population equivalent (the state's adjusted population divided by the number of members) was 50 percent, and the

Table A-9 Adjusted Populations of Virginia's Congressional Districts in the Eighth Congress (1803–1805)

District Number	Adjusted Population
1	25,438
2	28,514
3	35,986
4	36,418
5	29,821
6	37,872
7	39,980
8	33,451
9	32,988
10	36,057
11	34,891
12	42,327
13	29,922
14	35,655
15	36,403
16	31,677
17	34,139
18	29,795
19	32,904
20	33,228
21	31,126
22	33,243

Sources: "Mapping Early American Elections," Eighth Congress (1803–1805); U.S. Bureau of the Census, *Population of States and Counties of the United States: 1790–1990* (March 1996); and U.S. Bureau of the Census, *Return of the Whole Number of Persons within the Several Districts of the United States*, 1800 Census of Population.

ratio of the largest-populated district to the smallest-populated district was 1.66. Neither of these comes close to complying with today's requirements for congressional districts. (If these calculations were based on the number of whole persons, the results are considerably worse, with the percentage of the ideal being 66 percent and the ratio being 2.02.)

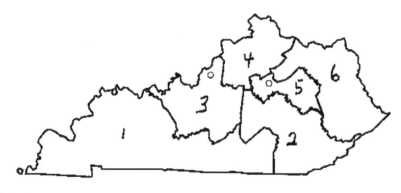

Kentucky

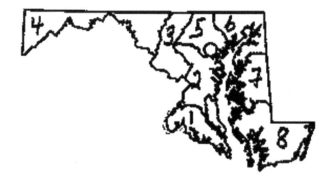

Maryland

North Carolina

Figure A-1 Eighth Congress (1803–1805): Districts for Kentucky, Maryland, and North Carolina.

Note: A small circle on a map indicates a city.

Source: Derived from "Mapping Early American Elections."

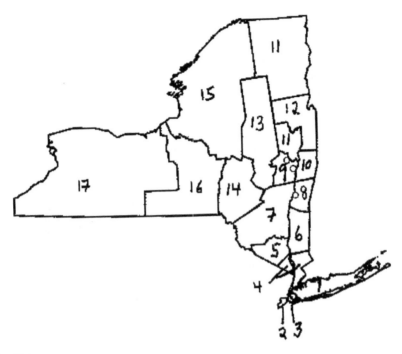

New York

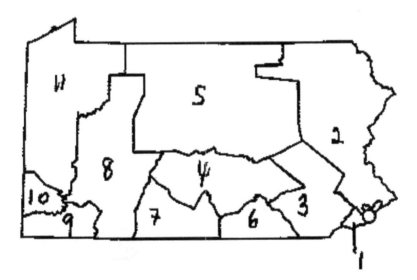

Pennsylvania

Figure A-2   Eighth Congress (1803–1805): Districts in New York and Pennsylvania.

Note: A small circle on a map indicates a city.

Source: Derived from "Mapping Early American Elections."

South Carolina

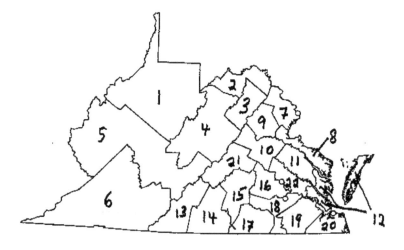

Virginia

Figure A-3 Eighth Congress (1803–1805): Districts in South Carolina and Virginia.

Note: A small circle on a map indicates a city.
Source: Derived from "Mapping Early American Elections."

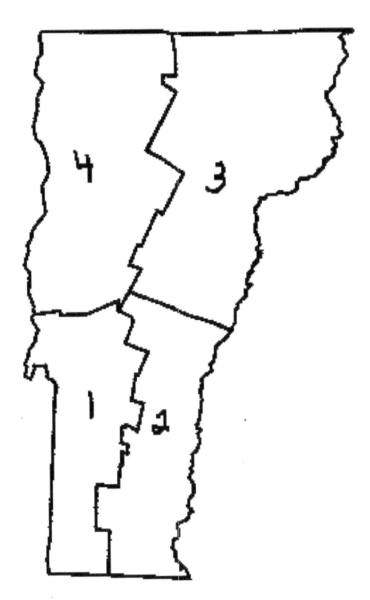

Figure A-4 Eighth Congress (1803–1805): Districts in Vermont.

Note: A small circle on a map indicates a city.

Source: Derived from "Mapping Early American Elections."

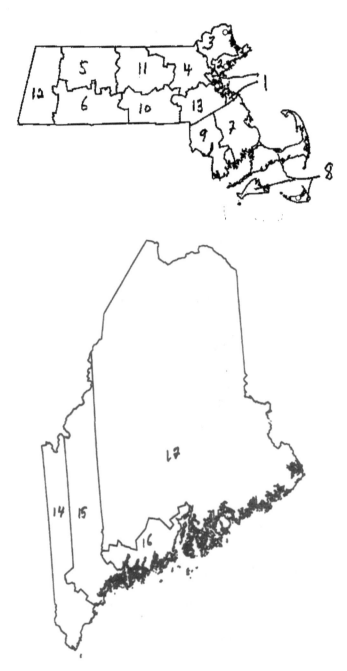

Figure A-5   Eighth Congress (1803–1805): Districts in Massachusetts, Including What Is Today the State of Maine.

Note: A small circle on a map indicates a city.

Source: Derived from "Mapping Early American Elections."

Appendix B

Occurrences of Certain Provisions Regarding State Legislative or Congressional Redistricting in Each State's Constitution as of June 2019

The presence of a provision is indicated by a "Y."

State	Presence of Provision for					State Constitution's Reference
	Pennsylvania's Free and Equal Elections Clause	Requiring Free Elections	Requiring Compactness	Requiring Contiguity	Requiring Equal Population	
Alabama				Y	Y	Section 200
Alaska				Y	Y	Art. VI, § 6
Arizona	Y		Y	Y	Y	Art. II, § 21; Art. IV, § 14
Arkansas	Y		Y	Y	Y	Art. 3, §2; Art. 8
California			Y	Y	Y	Art. XXI, § 2
Colorado		Y	Y	Y	Y	Art. II, §5; Art. V, §§ 46 and 47
Connecticut				Y	Y	Art. Third, §§ 3–6
Delaware	Y			Y	Y	Art I, § 3; Art. II, § 2 A
Florida			Y	Y	Y	Art. III, §§ 16, 20, and 21
Georgia				Y		Art. III, § II
Hawaii			Y	Y	Y	Art. IV, § 6
Idaho				Y	Y	Art. III, § 5
Illinois	Y		Y	Y	Y	Art. III, § 3; Art. IV, § 3
Indiana	Y			Y	Y	Art. II, § 1; Art. IV, § 5
Iowa						None
Kansas						None

State					Provision
Kentucky	Y		Y	Y	Sections 6 and 33
Louisiana				Y	Art. III, § 6
Maine			Y	Y	Art. IV, Part First, § 2; Art. IV, Part Second, § 2
Maryland		Y	Y	Y	Declaration of Rights, Art. 7; Art. III, § 4
Massachusetts		Y	Y	Y	Part the First, Art. IX; Amendment Art. CI
Michigan		Y	Y	Y	Art. IV, § 6, par. 13
Minnesota			Y	Y	Art. IV, §§ 2 and 3
Mississippi			Y	Y	Art. 13, § 254
Missouri		Y	Y	Y	Art. I, § 25; Art. III, § 3
Montana		Y	Y	Y	Art. II, § 13; Art. V, § 14
Nebraska		Y	Y	Y	Art. I, § 22; Art. III, § 5
Nevada				Y	Art. III, § 5
New Hampshire		Y	Y	Y	Part First, Art. 11; Part Second, Art. 9
New Jersey		Y	Y	Y	Art. IV, § 3
New Mexico		Y		Y	Art. II, § 8
New York		Y	Y	Y	Art. III, § 5
North Carolina		Y	Y	Y	Art. I, §10; Art. II, §§ 3 and 5
North Dakota		Y	Y	Y	Art. IV, § 2
Ohio		Y	Y	Y	Art. XI; Art XIX, § 2

(Continued)

State	Presence of Provision for					State Constitution's Reference
	Pennsylvania's Free and Equal Elections Clause	Requiring Free Elections	Requiring Compactness	Requiring Contiguity	Requiring Equal Population	
Oklahoma	Y					Art. III, § 5
Oregon	Y			Y	Y	Art. II, § 1; Art. IV, § 7
Pennsylvania	Y		Y	Y	Y	Art. I, § 5, Art. II, § 16
Rhode Island			Y		Y	Art. VII, § 1; Art. VIII, § 1
South Carolina						None
South Dakota	Y		Y	Y	Y	Art. VI, § 19; Art. III, § 5
Tennessee	Y				Y	Art. I, § 5; Art. II, § 4
Texas				Y	Y	Art. III, §§ 25 and 26
Utah		Y				Art. I, § 17e
Vermont		Y	Y	Y	Y	Chapter I, Art. 8; Chapter II, §§ 13, 18 and 55
Virginia		Y	Y	Y	Y	Art. I, § 6; Art. II, § 6
Washington	Y		Y	Y	Y	Art. I, § 19; Art. II, § 43
West Virginia			Y	Y	Y	Art. VI, § 4
Wisconsin			Y	Y	Y	Art. IV, § 3
Wyoming	Y					Art. I, § 27
Number of States with Provision	13	12	25	38	40	

Appendix C

Disparities in Apportionment Showing Congressional Districts in Each State Having Largest and Smallest Populations

State	1946 Population	1928 Population	1897 Population
AL	459,930 251,757	310,054 170,188	188,214 130,451
AZ	2 representatives—elected at large	1 representative	Not yet admitted
AR	423,152 177,476	330,292 180,348	220,261 147,806
CA	409,404 194,199	516,283 129,357	228,717 147,642
CO	322,412 172,847	281,170 140,532	207539 204,659
CT	450,189 247,601	336,027 224,426	248,582 121,792
DE	1 representative	1 representative	1 representative
FL	439,895 186,831	315,292 187,474	202,792 188,630
GA	487,552 235,420	308,364 205,343	180,300 135,948
ID	300,357 224,516	253,542 178,324	1 representative
IL	914,053 112,116	560,634 158,092	184,027 159,186
IN	460,926 241,323	348,061 179,737	191,472 139,359
IA	392,052 268,900	295,449 156,594	203,470 153,712

State			
KS	382,546	280,045	278,208
	249,574	152,378	167,314
KY	413,690	289,766	192,055
	225,426	168,067	141,461
LA	333,295	255,372	214,785
	240,166	204,909	152,025
ME	290,335	195,072	183,070
	276,695	188,563	153,778
MD	534,568	311,413	208,165
	195,427	194,568	153,912
MA	346,623	259,954	174,866
	278,459	217,307	169,418
MI	419,007	533,748	191,841
	200,265	198,679	148,626
MN	334,781	275,645	188,480
	283,845	112,235	184,848
MS	470,781	349,662	224,618
	201,316	177,185	143,315
MO	503,738	521,587	230,478
	214,787	138,807	152,442
MT	323,597	333,476	1 representative
	235,859	215,413	
NE	369,190	288,090	195,434
	305,961	173,458	163,674

(Continued)

State	1946 Population	1928 Population	1897 Population
NV	1 representative	1 representative	1 representative
NH	247,033 244,491	224,842 218,241	190,532 185,998
NJ	370,220 226,169	290,610 228,615	256,093 125,793
NM	2 representatives—elected at large	1 representative	Not yet admitted
NY	365,918 235,913	391,620 151,605	227,978 114,766
NC	358,573 239,040	408,139 202,760	204,686 160,288
ND	2 representatives—elected at large	220,700 210,203	1 representative
OH	698,650 163,561	439,013 167,217	205,293 158,027
OK	416,863 189,547	325,680 189,472	Not yet admitted
OR	355,099 210,991	346,989 160,502	158,205 155,562
PA	441,518 212,979	390,991 136,283	309,986 129,764
RI	374,463 338,883	210,201 193,176	180,548 164,958

SC	361,933 / 251,137	266,956 / 203,418	200,000 / 141,750
SD	485,829 / 157,132	251,405 / 138,031	1 representative
TN	388,938 / 225,918	290,396 / 145,403	199,972 / 153,773
TX	528,951 / 230,010	349,859 / 211,032	210,907 / 102,827
UT	293,922 / 256,388	229,907 / 219,489	2 representatives—elected at large
VT	1 representative	176,596 / 175,832	169,940 / 162,482
VA	360,679 / 243,165	312,458 / 167,588	187,467 / 145,536
WA	412,689 / 244,908	348,474 / 200,258	2 representatives—elected at large
WV	378,630 / 281,333	279,072 / 214,930	202,289 / 177,840
WI	391,467 / 263,088	276,503 / 214,206	187,001 / 149,845
WY	1 representative	1 representative	1 representative

Source: Appendix I to the opinion of the Supreme Court in *Colegrove v. Green*, 328 U.S. 549, 557–559 (1946).

References

Act . . . to provide for congressional redistricting, Pub. L. No. 90-196, 81 Stat. 581 (1967).

Apportionment Act of 1802, 2 Stat. 128, January 18, 1802.

Apportionment Act of 1842, Pub. L. 27-47, 5 Stat. 491.

Apportionment Act of 1850, Pub. L. 31-11, 9 Stat. 432.

Apportionment Act of 1872, Pub. L. 42-11, 17 Stat. 28.

Apportionment Act of 1882, Pub. L. 47-20, 22 Stat. 5.

Apportionment Act of 1891, Pub. L. 51-116, 26 Stat. 735.

Apportionment Act of 1901, Pub. L. 56-93, 31 Stat. 733.

Apportionment Act of 1911, Pub. L. 62-5, 37 Stat. 13.

Apportionment Act of 1929, 46 Stat. 21, Ch. 28, § 21.

Baker v. Carr, 369 U.S. 186 (1962).

Bandemer v. Davis, 603 F. Supp. 1479 (S.D. Ind. 1984).

Benisek v. Lamone, 585 U.S. _____ (2018) (slip opinion accessed at https://www.supremecourt.gov/opinions/17pdf/17-333_b97c.pdf on November 11, 2019) (Benisek).

Benisek v. Lamone, 348 F. Supp. 3d 493 (MD 2018). Also known as Case No. 1:13-cv-03233-JKB, United States District Court for the District of Maryland, decided November 7, 2018 (*Benisek v. Lamone* District Court on Merits). Opinion accessed via casetext.com through scotusblog on June 14, 2019.

Bolling v. Sharpe, 347 U.S. 497 (1954).

Brief of Common Cause Appellees, *Rucho v. Common Cause*, Supreme Court of the United States, No. 18-422 (March 4, 2019).

Broom v. Wood, 1 F. Supp. 134 (1932) (the district court decision reviewed by the Supreme Court in *Wood v. Broom*).

Chen, Jowei, and Jonathan Rodden. 2015. "Cutting Through the Thicket: Redistricting Simulations and the Detection of Partisan Gerrymanders." *Election Law Journal* 14: 331–45.

Colegrove v. Green, 328 U.S. 529 (1946).

Coleman v. Miller, 307 U.S. 433 (1939).

Common Cause v. Lewis, North Carolina, Wake County, General Court of Justice, Superior Court Division, No. 18 CVS 14001, Judgment (September 3, 2019) (*Common Cause v. Lewis* Judgment). Accessed at http://www.commoncause.org/north-carolina/wp-content/uploads/sites/22/2019/09/Common-Cause

-v.-Lewis-trial-court-decision-9.3.19.pdf on January 6, 2020, through the Brennan Center for Justice.

Common Cause v. Lewis, North Carolina, Wake County, General Court of Justice, Superior Court Division, No. 18 CVS 14001, Remedial Order (October 28, 2019) (*Common Cause v. Lewis* Remedial Order). Accessed at https://www.common cause.org/wp-content/uploads/2019/10/10.28.19-Order-approving-remedial -districts.pdf on January 7, 2019, through the Brennan Center for Justice.

Common Cause v. Lewis, Supreme Court of North Carolina, order denying application for discretionary appeal, November 15. 2019. Accessed at https://www .brennancenter.org/sites/default/files/2019-11/2019-11-15-Order.pdf on January 20, 2019, through the Brennan Center for Justice.

Common Cause v. Rucho, 318 F. Supp. 3d 777 (MDNC 2018). Also referred to as No. 1:16-CV-1026; No. 1:16-CV-1164 Memorandum Opinion (M.D.N.C. August 27, 2018). Accessed via casetext.com on June 15, 2019.

Crocker, Royce. 2012. *Congressional Redistricting: An Overview*. Washington, DC: Congressional Research Service.

Davis v. Bandemer, 478 U.S. 109 (1986).

Evenwel v. Abbott, 578 U.S. _____ (2016).

Gaffney v. Cummings, 412 U.S. 735 (1973).

Gill v. Whitford, 585 U.S. _____ (2018) (slip opinion accessed at https://www .supremecourt.gov/opinions/17pdf/16-1161_dc8f.pdf on November 11, 2019).

Gomillion v. Lightfoot, 363 U.S. 338 (1960).

Gray v. Sanders, 372 U.S. 368 (1963).

Grove, Tara Leigh. 2015. "The Lost History of the Political Question Doctrine." *N.Y.U. Law R.* 90: 1908.

Hacker, Andrew. 1964. *Congressional Districting: The Issue of Equal Representation* (rev. ed.). Washington, DC: Brookings Institution.

Harper v. Lewis, North Carolina, Wake County, General Court of Justice, Superior Court Division, No. 19 CVS o12667 (October 28, 2019). Accessed at https:// www.brennancenter.org/sites/default/files/2019-10/2019-10-28-Harper%20 v_%20Lewis-Order.pdf on January 8, 2020.

Harris v. Arizona Independent Redistricting Commission, 578 U.S. ___ (2016) (lip opinion accessed at https://www.supremecourt.gov/opinions/15pdf/14-232_ihdj.pdf).

Harvard Law Review. 2019. "Political Question, Public Rights, and Sovereign Immunity." 130: 723.

Karcher v. Daggett, 462 U.S. 725 (1983).

Kennett v. Chambers, 55 U.S. (14 How.) 38 (1852).

Kirkpatrick v. Preisler, 394 U.S. 526 (1969).

League of Women Voters of Pennsylvania v. Commonwealth of Pennsylvania, 175 A. 3d 282 (Pa. 2018) (Initial Order of January 22, 2018). Page references in text are to a copy of the opinion on the Brennan Center website downloaded on June 2, 2019, from https://www.brennancenter.org/legal-work/league-women-voters -v-pennslyvania.

League of Women Voters of Pennsylvania v. Commonwealth of Pennsylvania, 178 A. 3d 737 (Pa. 2018) (Opinion of February 7, 2018). Page references in text are to a copy of the opinion on the Brennan Center website downloaded on April 11, 2019, from https://www.brennancenter.org/legal-work/league-women-voters -v-pennslyvania.

League of Women Voters of Pennsylvania v. Commonwealth of Pennsylvania, 181 A. 3d 1083 (Pa. 2018) (Remedy on February 19, 2018). Page references in text are to a copy of the opinion on the Brennan Center website downloaded on April 11, 2019, from https://www.brennancenter.org/legal-work/ league-women-voters-v-pennslyvania.

League of Women Voters of Pennsylvania v. Commonwealth of Pennsylvania, Court Remedial Plan 2 19, Measures of Compactness. From the Brennan Center website downloaded on January 19, 2020, from https://drive.google.com /file/d/1r8i35PtxqZ8Rdh6DZT4fp-sNB57MCc4J/view.

Luther v. Borden, 48 U.S. (7 How.) 1, (1849).

Mahan v. Howell, 410 U.S. 678 (1973).

"Mapping Early American Elections," 8th Congress (1803–1805), maps and information on methods (single representative, multimember, or at large elections) for the First through Nineteenth Congresses located at earlyamericanelections .org/maps.

Marbury v. Madison, 1 Cranch 137 (1803).

Mulry, Mary. 2006. "Summary of Accuracy and Coverage Evaluation for Census 2000." Research Report Series Statistics #2006-3 (February 28). Washington, DC: United States Bureau of the Census.

Nixon v. Herndon, 273 U.S. 536 (1927).

O'Neil, Cathy. 2016. *Weapons of Math Destruction: How Big Data Increases Inequality and Threatens Democracy*. New York: Crown.

Pacific States Telephone & Telegraph Co. v. Oregon, 223 U.S. 118 (1912).

Polsby, Daniel D., and Robert D. Popper. 1991. "The Third Criterion: Compactness as a Procedural Safeguard Against Partisan Gerrymandering." *Yale Law and Policy Review* 9: 301–53 (1991).

Rawls, John. 1971. *A Theory of Justice*. Cambridge, MA: Harvard University Press.

Reock, Earnest C. 1961. "Note: Measuring Compactness as a Requirement of Legislative Apportionment." *Midwest Journal of Political Science* 5: 70–74.

Reynolds v. Sims, 377 U.S. 533 (1964).

Rogers v. Lodge, 458 U.S. 613 (1982).

Rucho v. Common Cause and *Lamone v. Benisek* (2019) (slip opinions of majority and of dissent accessed at https://www.supremecourt.gov/opinions/18pdf /18-422_9oll.pdf on November 11, 2019).

Trimble v. Gordon, 430 U.S. 762 (1977).

United States Bureau of the Census. 1982–1986. *Congressional Districts of the 98th Congress*. 1980 Census of Population. Various dates with a separate report for each state and corrected reports issued for certain states, Table 1.

United States Bureau of the Census. 1962. *Population of Congressional Districts for 88th Congress, April 1, 1960,* 1960 Census of Population: Supplementary Report No. PC(S1)-26.

United States Bureau of the Census. 1996. *Population of States and Counties of the United States: 1790–1990.*

United States Bureau of the Census. n.d. *Return of the Whole Number of Persons within the Several Districts of the United States.* 1800 Census of Population.

United States Constitution.

United States v. Holliday. 70 U.S. (3 Wall.) 407 (1866).

Vickery, William. 1961. "On the Prevention of Gerrymandering." *Political Science Quarterly* 76: 105–10.

Vieth v. Jubelirer, 541 U.S. 267 (2004).

Vieth v. Pennsylvania, 188 F. Supp. 2d 532 (MD Pa. 2002).

Washington, George. 1796. "Farewell Address." See https://www.ourdocuments .gov/doc.php?flash=false&doc=15&page=transcript, viewed on January 1, 2010.

Wesberry v. Sanders, 376 U.S. 1 (1964).

Whitcomb v. Chavis, 403 U.S. 124 (1971).

White v. Register, 412 U.S. 755 (1973).

Williams v. Suffolk Ins. Co., 38 U.S. (13 Pet.) 415 (1839).

Wood v. Broom, 287 U. S. 1 (1932).

Yoshino, Kenji. 2011. "The New Equal Protection." *Harv. L. Rev.* 124: 747.

Index

First Amendment rights, 28, 49–51, 76
Florida
    disparities in apportionment in, 100
    redistricting plans in, as of
        June 2019, 96
Forsyth-Yadkin, 61
Fortas, Abraham, 35
"for want of jurisdiction," 7
Fourteenth Amendment, 1, 8, 10,
    15–16, 22, 23, 25, 28, 30, 54
Frankfurter, Felix, 14–15, 35
Free and Equal Elections Clause
    (Pennsylvania), 42–44, 47, 96–98
Free Elections Clause
    (North Carolina), 58

G
Gaffney v. Cummings, 25, 50
Georgia
    disparities in apportionment in,
        13–15, 100
    House of Representatives
        apportioned in, 79
    one-person, one-vote rule and, 16
    redistricting plans in, as of
        June 2019, 96
    statewide at-large elections of House
        members in, 80
    violation of Equal Protection Clause
        and, 31
Gerry, Elbridge, 27, 39
gerrymandering, 27–62
    applicability of Equal Protection
        Clause to, 32
    constitutionality of, xi
    definition of, xi
    income-based, xi, 28, 32, 56, 57, 63
    justiciable claims, xi, 33, 36, 53,
        55–56, 77
    manageable standards for resolving,
        9, 33, 55, 63–73, 75–76
    nonjusticiable claims, 37, 53, 54,
        77–78
    occupation-based, xi, 28, 32, 56, 57
    partisan, 32–36, 42–43, 48–49, 53, 55,
        58–59, 78
    racial, 22, 23, 28–29, 31, 61–62

    violation of equal protection in,
        32–34, 59
    violation of North Carolina
        Constitution, 58–62, 65, 71
Gill v. Whitford, 48
Ginsberg, Ruth Bader, 36
Gomillion v. Lightfoot, 28–29, 35, 39
Gray v. Sanders, 16, 22
Guarantee Clause, 6–7, 8
Guilford, 61, 72

H
Harper v. Lewis, 61
*Harris v. Arizona Independent
    Redistricting Commission*, 52
Hawaii, redistricting plans in, as of
    June 2019, 96
heightened scrutiny, 22, 32
House districts, 59–60, 61, 72

I
Idaho
    disparities in apportionment in, 100
    redistricting plans in, as of
        June 2019, 96
Illinois
    congressional voting districts in, 7
    disparities in apportionment
        in, 100
    redistricting plans in, as of
        June 2019, 96
    violation of Equal Protection Clause
        and, 30, 32–33
income-based gerrymandering, xi, 28,
    32, 56, 57, 63
incumbency protection, 45–46, 70–73
Indiana
    disparities in apportionment in, 100
    redistricting plans in, as of
        June 2019, 96
intentional discrimination,
    requirement of, 31–34, 44, 76
intermediate zone, 68–70, 78
Iowa
    disparities in apportionment in, 100
    redistricting plans in, as of
        June 2019, 96

J

Jackson, Robert, 7
judicially discoverable and
    manageable standards, 9, 33, 55,
    63–73, 75–76
justice, Rawls's theory of, 57
justiciability doctrine, 5

K

Kagan, Elena, 53
Kansas
    disparities in apportionment in, 101
    redistricting plans in, as of
      June 2019, 96
Karcher v. Daggett, 18–19, 22, 32–33,
    37–38
Kennedy, Anthony, 35–36, 49, 78
Kennett v. Chambers, 6
Kentucky
    adjusted populations of
      congressional districts in, following
      1800 Census, 38, 81
    disparities in apportionment in, 101
    Eighth Congress districts for,
      following 1800 Census, 90
    House of Representatives
      apportioned in, 79
    redistricting plans in, as of
      June 2019, 97
Kirkpatrick v. Preisler, 17–18, 35

L

League of Women Voters of Pennsylvania v.
    Commonwealth of Pennsylvania,
    39–47, 71
Louisiana
    disparities in apportionment in, 101
    redistricting plans in, as of
      June 2019, 97
Luther v. Borden, 6

M

Mahan v. Howell, 24
Maine
    disparities in apportionment in, 101
    redistricting plans in, as of
      June 2019, 97

malapportionment, 39, 76
manageable standards, 9–10, 33, 53, 55,
    63–73, 75–78
Marbury v. Madison, 5
Maryland
    adjusted populations of
      congressional districts in, following
      1800 Census, 38, 81–82
    disparities in apportionment in, 101
    Eighth Congress districts for,
      following 1800 Census, 90
    House of Representatives
      apportioned in, 79
    redistricting plans in, as of
      June 2019, 97
Massachusetts, 94
    adjusted populations of
      congressional districts in, following
      1800 Census, 38, 82–83
    House of Representatives
      apportioned in, 79
    redistricting plans in, as of
      June 2019, 97
Mattingly, Jonathan, 52
Michigan
    disparities in apportionment in, 101
    redistricting plans in, as of
      June 2019, 97
Minnesota
    disparities in apportionment in, 101
    redistricting plans in, as of
      June 2019, 97
Mississippi
    disparities in apportionment
      in, 101
    redistricting plans in, as of
      June 2019, 97
Missouri, disparities in apportionment
    in, 101
modern doctrine of political
    question, 9
Montana
    disparities in apportionment in, 101
    redistricting plans in, as of
      June 2019, 97
mootness, 8
multimember legislative districts, 30